# Takes Guts and Years Sometimes

Linda Lerner

NY Books™

The New York Quarterly Foundation, Inc.
New York, New York

NYQ Books™ is an imprint of The New York Quarterly Foundation, Inc.

The New York Quarterly Foundation, Inc.
P. O. Box 2015
Old Chelsea Station
New York, NY 10113

www.nyqbooks.org

First Edition

Set in New Baskerville

Layout and Design by Raymond P. Hammond
Cover Illustration by Angela Mark and Michael Shores
Shark Art Studios | sharkart.com

Library of Congress Control Number: 2011926466

ISBN: 978-1-935520-31-3

# Takes Guts and Years Sometimes

# Takes Guts and Years Sometimes

*in memory of my parents,*

*Frieda & Philip Lerner,*

*and of my partner,*

*Andrew Gettler*

# Contents

## New and Uncollected Poems

## For Leo Connellan

**from *Because You Can't I Will* (2005)**

**from *City Woman* (2006)**

**from *Living in Dangerous Times* (2007)**

**from _Something Is Burning in Brooklyn_ (2009)**

New & Uncollected Poems

# Takes Guts and Years Sometimes

she was generation x/pretty
buying sneakers in footlocker/greenwich village
as i was   on my way
to a poetry reading...
*nice*  i said of the black & white pair she tried on
an ugly   clunky one in her hand   *i don't want nice...pretty*
*i want ugly*
quietly slamming thru a generation barrier
so fast i missed it...

the poet spoke of using slang
when it took courage to
fuck with words on the page
not give a shit
ground breaking anarchist in her youth
generation before mine
chose black not pink
village hole in the wall jazz
to carnegie hall classical

old enough to be that teen's grandmother
& that other kid's
who ran wild with red   purple crayons in school
ran to the window when bored
ran thoughts past pedagogical heads
kid i abandoned for many years
to curl hair against its natural bent
breath in the confines of textbook grammar

till i got back her nerve
& stuck out my verbal tongue at robotic minds
scribbling graffiti over dull
whitewashed thoughts   pastel anything
trashing commas   periods
took years before i could confidently
say: I choose ugly

17

## Before the First Initiation

graffiti is the rap poets' slam
louder than words we've been fed
to spit out so we won't end up
        homeless or worse
all the soft toned polite acceptable
a rock band's blast kids hunger for
without knowing why
        silences...
I am grateful for every
angry lined crazy color let loose
             on walls
every off the beat voice
        that gets out
tastes the sound of freedom
lets someone feel
what being born REALLY means
before the first intimation
of an ending

# If I'm Lucky

sometimes I can feel the words
as I feel & smell a lover's body
as I feel the day waking
though my window
coffee brewing words
I inhale as my cat rubs
a new morning against me
& with all the lost luxury of youth
let go of caution
shoot words all over the page
as through a paint gun
& the man   if he's still here
might be sneaking a call
to someone who slips past me
to the page
I'm late for work
there are chores
but the only thing that matters
the words   to hear what they're trying
to say   not mean
feel them on my tongue
as I feel him   as
I feel the first morning air
as I breathe

# The Insult of Good Intentions

I refuse a seat someone offers me
insulted    as if    what?
the empress has no clothes
my image abruptly aged by a twenty something thief
ridiculous
               and yet...
little things that keep happening, well intended
but it's my choice:
to pay a higher price at the cinema
stand on the longer line
tip more than I can afford
pretend the man I'm with will rescue me
when the economic bottom separates
like that huge chunk of ice in the atlantic
foreshadowing what imagination bumps against
in sleepless nights
                      my choice
to spend what I don't have for
what the entitlement of birth grants:
to prove that I am more than my job description
on a w2 form, a number on a certificate
I am spending to buy back years
lost in scared & reckless youth
ten more years to create that masterpiece,
see in a man's eyes what my lover saw when
he first fell into mine,
years before I'll take that seat

## Riding on a Late Night Amtrak
## Back to New York from Philly

on a voice flatlining days
across stock options   numbers
reaching toward infinity
I'm riding thru a businessman's America
the flattest country I've ever seen—
modern technology has created
what the prairie must have once
looked like to westerners a century or two ago
cleared of horses   sagebrush
not even a saloon or knockdown fight
not one human visible

# Visions of Outlaw Ghosts

they shoot their way out of death
in post offices   slip
thru cracks nobody sees widening
sees beneath masks
billy the kid   dillinger hiding out
in backalley art   whispering
to poets/bluesmen   comeback on
album covers & t-shirts
the skeleton with a rose between his teeth/

civil servants sorting/carrying
letters   parcels   cramming
them into holes

bukowski   ten years with
a leather sack on his back
the worst routes because
he *had a vocabulary*
wouldn't bend under the stone
boss/mr. stone

would have killed someone every day
taken that pony express ride in
Denver   New York   New Jersey
post offices throughout America
to deliver his message: another
disgruntled employee
holding dullness hostage

if he hadn't been a drifter
taken up squatter's rights
on the page
fired away when
the stone came down too hard
barely room even to breathe
hear the brothers calling to him
to whisper back:
deliver his life

# Here's the Catch

let's do catch up, somebody says:
If I could catch my breath
catch my life like a magic ball, catch on that fast
to keep the ball, the catch in the too good
to be true that is, like catching a shooting star
outside the song, catch in my voice
that keeps it from flying
to catch the day by its roots every day
a good catch my mother always said
of what always gets away
my cat caught: a string hanging
from his mouth I couldn't pull out
and glimpsing the tail end of his catch
I mistook for a toy, tricked him with food
to drop, then caught the enormity of his catch:
way he stared at the spot where
the mouse I had gargbaged lay
this mouse that was big as the great marlin
Hemingway's old man caught and lost without loosing

## What Won't Die Easily

the old year lines sidewalks
waiting to be garbaged, pieces of pine
broken off scattered underfoot,
needles too soft to draw blood
get beneath nails, stick to clothes
an irritation, like the insult of indifference
the thought: If I vanished, how long
before someone alive would notice;

unable to flesh ghosts, they recede not vanish,
what has gone and never had
hard to get rid of...

trees hauled away, quickly replaced,
days, months of one year
another begins to claim,
nothing to tell me it's a new year;
the heart beats the same resolution

# Just Watch

*(Merce Cunningham concert at*
*Rockefeller Park, 8/1/09)*

it is not like anything else because
there is no such thing here as like
so forget it—
before you can trap them
watch them move out of story
I'd say like the breath if
it were possible and wishing it were
as you watch how the breath propels
their every move, together or apart
leaf colored blazing red hot fleeting
blue against the musicing sounds
that never cease you no longer hear
and has nothing to do with them or you
who've given up trying to capture
them with intricate plots, you just watch
stretched out on your blanket on
that huge expanse of grassy present

# Following a Professor into Blues Waters Stalls on Dry Land

because how can he send his words
screamin' & cryin' thru the Mississippi Delta
'bout some pretty momma

tenured language he's given his life for
this balding professor who wants us to see
what drives him howlin' naked
behind that verbal wall
he's led us too...

halfway into the lecture, we're
still waiting
what is it about Muddy Waters,
Robert Johnson, Leadbelly moves him
in his dark suit starched white shirt
to get down and dirty with them
struggles as hard as he can
only nothing   not a speck of dirt...

he takes us to a bar in a two street town
on the edge of nowhere
we've never been

seedy looking joint, a bunch of
guys jammin' something we can't hear
he opens the door a crack   puts one foot in
they give him a look   you know the one
scared shit & pretending not to be

turns around and begins
fiddling with a machine

a guitar twangs out
an acoustic harp drums a piano
so clear I can see past the room this day
every sound paints where
he's been leading us

the professor closes his eyes...
curls smokey voiced around him
we are gone from the seats
our bodies are occupying

*It's hard but it's fun*
blueslady sings
*life may break your little heart*
                *baby oh baby*
the professor is rocking back & forth

*please don't feel so bad*
*makes daddy feel so bad*
*baby oh baby...*

## What Remains

my business is words
but i've another language
my poems only approximate
a sound picked up
like my lover's scent
that spoke to me hours
after he left...
voice is what this language
                is about
and touch and smell/that
lives in alphabet
and has none

# They Were Never the Wallendas

down the echo of a bard's howl
where once they sang
       *times they are a changin'*
to middle class childhoods
greeted Christ on a motorcycle and
fucked the system in pre-AIDS America
they still fuck: young disciples
who remind them of someone they once knew,
cautious lust from safe-house neighborhoods
dull husbands to pay like
the parents or friends before them...

wild talk sold a lot of images:
men who took off on the same howl, got
drunk on Buk Beer, ran with
imaginary bulls in Pamplona
reincarnated Papa for
a moment in imagination;
how many starry nights by
the East river did i flee with them
from Mexican police, bulls, girlfriend of a
guerrilla fighter in some third world country...

another river   the Hudson
another time...

i've met people who've slept
beneath bridges   scrounged
garbage cans for food
sick with diarrhea for days
prayed for a bed in a shelter
to make it thru: one more night
chose freedom over pensioned death
gave up everything to be
with one they loved;
wasn't those wild talkin' men and women

their mid-age warnings now
when i take up with a homeless poet of love

a new road and don't ask:  to  where
how much   to what end...

## See, I Told You

fear leapt off roofs in 1930's flashback
leaving her homeless, alone to raise two kids
when my father's rage at his boss, a job he hated
exploded and sent her running for cover,
this housewife camouflaged a soldier whose quiet street
sudden noise turned into a combat zone:

fear rising from boiling water
kept her shutting off lights after us,
scraping crumbs off plates to seal for reuse
watering down milk and juice:

It was war—war without discharge,
no one could convince her the depression ended
decades ago, that it wasn't an illusion
and any moment banks wouldn't start closing
century old businesses fail, the market start plunging
and news of some bankrupt family men jumping
into death's insurance safety net—

when something's over doesn't mean it's finished;
the years were breadlines she stood on
waiting patiently for that vindication
I wish in an absurd crazy kind of way
she were here now to finally get:

*see, I told you,* she can't say,
but I still hear

# The Enemy

the way my cat rubs against someone
to pick up a scent he never forgets
I sniffed out my father's anger in a stranger
his eyes smoldering
from way in the back I could feel the heat
...anger that's the molasses black
of country nights nothing seeps thru—
my father   a Russian Jew
whose family didn't make it out
and I never bridged the hurt/blame
his death now makes it safe to cross

when this man from Palestine
stands up to speak:  his words
don't all get thru the noise
but enough: Israel is being hit
Jews killed in retribution

damn this stranger
what have I do with a country
I never wanted to visit a religion I don't follow
wayward child a father mourned as
he shouted   *no daughter of mine*   thru his fears

I rush out of the room...
homes are burning in a foreigner's eyes
planes shot down
blood soaked tears fill the space between us:
geography has become irrelevant

# The Scream

the bump that blue-purple's skin after a fall
when a mosquito bite is scratched yelling red
or death lurks its tumor head up to full zero color
is the scream I could feel all month
snake like shedding its colors behind

> *sorry*
> *it's all right*
> *doesn't matter*
> *shit happens*

and like the 20 inch steam pipe
which burst in Manhattan spewing forth
decades of rock   metal   asbestos debris
imagine one day I'll be walking down the street
alone or with a friend
an ordinary day like any other
and suddenly gripped with fear
feel that scream rush thru the city

I'll race after it but will never find
what I've stopped feeling to reclaim

a day just like that one
an ordinary day...

# Fault-lines

a Calif. friend told me he sometimes wakes
to his night table rattling
sees a street he's walking down wave,
holds his breath: *you get used to it,* he said

I live in N.Y. not Calif., I told him
faults crisscross the city
and maybe once in a hundred years
I lied...

like geologists, I'd mapped fault lines of vulnerability
  what was and wasn't likely
...just a job, boss I'd never quite got on with
wouldn't miss...friend like a brother
a pal, not a soul thing, and when
a father a mother were hospitalized
well, everyone must die sometime
retrofitted my life

until language shifted one Sept. morning,
Thanksgiving eve, in late May
and a word that meant one thing included another
so everything became like this or that
wrecking boundaries...

when buildings crumbled and thousands
were swallowed by the earth in China
screams spilled out of words too small to hold them...

listen, in the time it takes to pour a morning cup of coffee,
I've felt the earth shake, and tremors from quakes
never registered...

# The Period Keeps Receding the Harder She Tries to Reach It & the Closer She Gets

(A professor's essay assignment includes a list of rhetorical signposts, two of which must be in every paragraph.)

feels like trudging thru six feet of snow
to move down the page toward
the good looking young Russian
from her mother's album and
connect him with her father—
a dash won't do, looks forced,
her professor's disapproval
burns like the cold as the wind whips out
her father's disappointments—

*that child never listens*
*doesn't learn*

ranting about this country's counterfeit promises,
selling his breath for minimum wage freedom
she silences with a semicolon

but fails to make a smooth transition
slips several spaces into a Kiev village—
a young man with thick auburn hair
is being forced to join a band of disheveled youths
marching out of the country
*to save your life,* a voice cries
after him...*for freedom*

what freedom, she thinks
struggling to add one more appositive
remove the third prepositional phrase
come up with two subordinating conjunctions
replace one denotation with connotation
forgets about the black ice danger in language,
slips and falls into something else:

her father and the professor are
lined up against her in her own essay!

she bites down on her anger like a gag
to keep from screaming—
she starts over: same journey
freer climate,

failure has brought her closer
only she doesn't know it yet;
that's as far as she can go for now...

# Building in the Green

(Oct. 2008)


They came with saws, drills, a truckload of illegals
and plenty of 1990's cash...

an old couple, their two family house vanished
as I slept...green disappeared in the green
that pushed up a building thru neighbors' anger
thru the dusty noise ignorance purified;

jackhammering echoed thru the city
crossing state lines; everyone waited for
this building that resembled every other one
going up to be finished;

a tree centuries old lay on the dead grass
behind a fence separating that property from
where I lived, leaving a concrete area
I looked out on, everything

cold, hard, and gray,
felt like November in March, April, any month
of that year, the next and the one after;

when green shoots rose up
through cracks so small it didn't seem possible
came up through a drain hole

a sudden flowering of weeds, morning glories
broke thru the unfenced sides
tangled on the cellar banister where
cats lined up to be fed, eyeing the squirrels,
and sparrows perched on overhead wires;

is there such a thing as green sunshine
green silence?

some days no workers came where once
half a dozen; arguments broke out
among the builders, rumors of green drying up,
green teasing them everywhere they looked

and then   can you hear it...that crash
like a tree felled, only louder, much louder

# City Streets

## 1. The Same

happens every Sunday
on the same corner
I pass after having breakfast
with a man I call my friend,
a person small like a child
crouched down with her back to me
feeding the pigeons
always in the same position,
same restaurant where
the waiters ask if we want the usual, and
one or the other might request bacon this time
or change from sunny side to scrambled
and back again, every sun, and always
with her back to me, the same scene
like a piece of film cut off,
a failure in the mechanism
that keeps it going, and
having grown used to seeing it
I never think of the alternative
and how much older he is than I am

## 2. Beggars, Both

I hate seeing his artificial leg
by the subway stairs
when he's not there, throned
in his wheelchair,
a nasty man picking fights,
muttering obscenities...
would be so easy to throw a few coins
in his cup, feel good doing it
and forget about him
except I wouldn't...
he can't see by my refusal
to catch his eye
acknowledge what he's muttering
I'm begging him
to make me care about him;
it's an awful thing
to lose a leg, be poor
no longer young...
it was like that with my father
whose anger whipped me speechless,
places that revealed no scares
hurt for years...
when he died, tears begged
a dead man for something
I couldn't name;
I've heard people say
they won't speak ill of the dead, but
it's not the dead at all
we're speaking of. Or crying for.
Not the beggar holding out a cup
we're giving to....

### 3. Woman In the Box

could have been a man or woman
bundled outside the Jay Street station
for all I cared rushing to work
and didn't think much about
except to note its presence
when I saw that person
a friend said was a woman
accept clothes from a passerby
saw her drinking coffee
and writing in a small pad
every day writing in that same pad—
that's when she began to disappear
and a homeless Emily Dickinson
emerged in her place,
my great discovery; excited
and determined to help her
prepared to be astonished
by her uncultivated genius, when
I looked down at the pad
the box she kept outlining
in thick blue lines
securing the place where
that other woman lay forgotten,
bundled in clichés

# The City Feeds Me Hungry

back to the streets
every few years   graffiti walled free spoken
morality cleanses & depending on which
side of the alphabet street I'm job seeking on
learn to navigate my way
down the correct language
for what will pay the rent
on an apartment that doesn't exist
at that price
my mother's warning:
the more you get the more you want
about sex...becomes about everything now
urgent need replaces want
I've walked miles of cyber hot paved concrete
burning the skin off
my soul streets
till I feel the full moon
on a blazing hot summer's day
sitting in an outdoor cafe drinking coffee
walked out the loneliness
that's not as bad
since my lover unfantasized
& worse since he slipped back
streets on which I've sheltered
someone from death in poems
I cannot write enough of to keep him breathing
pulled off Houdini escapes in
street jazz sounds that feed me till I'm famished
back where I started from
the wheel keeps turning

# Define Freedom   Try

*"Freedom's just another word for nothing left to lose..."*
*—from "Me and Bobby McGee" as sung by Janis Joplin*

*After seeing the show, "Who Shot Rock & Roll"*
*at the Brooklyn Museum*

he came from one of those Eastern European
hard to pronounce countries I kept mixing up as
we talked in a local cafe when someone
suddenly shouted it's free tonight
and he ran, us following down the steps
into the subway through
the great open doors, crossing borders
and time lines, past photos of young rock stars
who'd headlined our youth like checkpoints
we'd passed through into new freedom—

a woman started singing a Jefferson Airplane song
swaying out of her late 40's body, I saw the
girl she called Brooklyn trash, watched
people point, say, remember, and this is when
and how and where, a foreign world to
that man who'd once huddled with youths
in attics and basements, bootlegging freedom
from musical minefields, songs
twanged out of guitars, pounded on drums,
a holler of Freedom exploding
could have meant   nobody said aloud;

those photos didn't bring me back
to anything I cared to remember;

44

a boy who would have envied my freedom
didn't know that other country
parented by fears, mistrust I was born in
trapped in a body I didn't own till a man
gave it back to me, I learned how to be loved
to live in a free mind-zone

I wanted to ask him where he got the courage
to do what took me years
but realizing the utter absurdity of this analogy
kept quiet...

*see those very long lines we avoided,* he boasted, as we left
miraculously having gotten in the second the doors opened
before guards could rope us in

and I saw a man who keeps escaping from a country
he returns to, driven to prove he'd done what
he could do again
if...

## Mid East Sand Blows Thru Katz's Deli
## New Year's Day, 2010

hotter than the mustard on my
pastrami & rye hot as
it was burning cold outside
*how hot* I asked,
"you have no idea..."
a waiter just back from Afghanistan said,

snatching a quick break from a celebration
watched thick salami & roast beef sandwiches
plates piled with potato salad
thick sour pickles, huge knishes
rapidly vanishing from
New York's taste bud memories,
pass across the counter, crossing generations
line barely moving
and thirsting for Dr. Brown's cream soda
to wash down what hadn't yet been eaten

inched my way closer to what the man ahead of me
was telling the waiter, who nodded,
explosives going off between his roast beef
and sauerkraut   *orders for him and a friend*
*yes it's to go...three more days,*
words drawing lines in sand
around them...sand I now stood in
could taste   sand hotter than I ever imagined—
.

the one who'd just come back
and the other en route to Iraq
the one so nervous, jittery, the other
so calm...

"I have a job to do," he said
without looking at me,
"then I'll come home," spoken with
such surety, I didn't know what to say
and forcing my way in where
I didn't belong


said, "my late partner was in Vietnam"
flinging a grenade into the silence
I didn't hear go off till
too late...

## Only One

There is only one death,
one jolt of lightning strike
one that keeps happening
and each time the stomach
caves in the same
and each time it gets harder,
not the knowing there'll be another
but that one day, someone
a living creature we
shared breath with
will simply be gone

# Unless

I want to peel the skin off words
get something raw that hurts the eye
tears whose salt I could taste
strong as what lined my margarita glass
in Mexico City the first night he broke through
before anyone did, do it before the skin
gets too thick, words that bleed color
stain sheets

I want to jump off a cliff in a poem
that doesn't have to follow a period of mourning
something catastrophic happening,

but if that's what it will take
dare to risk whatever is left
of my virginity to do it, summon up
the strength once more—

someone who loved me
once wrote:
*when I go down*
*you'll go down with me*
*unless I save you*

*unless* swims like a floater in my eye now
teasing me out of mind:
unless I don't want to be saved
unless the choice is no longer mine

for Leo Connellan

# FOR LEO CONNELLAN,
## UNFINISHED BUSINESS

*"What can I leave for you to feel of me"*
                    —Leo Connellan

I.

    *I never tried so hard with anyone,*
                            you said...
A big man dwarfed by yourself, a vision
lived in the shadow of your own genius
the world never quite recognized enough:
underlying joke   but it wasn't
you knew just how good those Maine
lobsters you fished out of New York waters are.
And so did I...

        To be the best I could make myself
showed me McGrath's "used up" horses
Karl Shapiro's boy his first naked time
listened to "Cherry Alive" girl singing
above the bellowing career-poets
beards and gypsy skirts bopping in dim lit open mike cafes:
"I will always be me I will always be new,"
like taking an oath
that gift...and what a gift it is:
my own voice in my poems
to know it    and know it isn't for sale;

child I was   aimed to please:
worked hard   harder still

      *I never tried so hard with anyone...*

II.

April 1988:
your *First Selected Poems* just come…
"Mornings and I
must kill" out of an old seaman's mouth
grabbed me, wouldn't let go
on a crowded NYC subway
like you once rode, *"helpless…into this ground"*
in my own city for the first time

and I was hooked;
before I ever met the man
the poet, Connellan, who owned this world
took me through your Rockland, Maine, boyhood home
watched your "'baby's toyland,"
Old Orchard Beach Maine burn down…

…A man retching in the grip of "doom booze"
not afraid to let me see you naked;

took your Staten Island Ferry through a city
I could only imagine
existed in my father's immigrant imagination
as it passed a Lady with a Torch:
to own his breath
the very breath he never knew was fully his…
Crossed America with you
as "The Moon Now Flushed" on a world
that hadn't yet burst apart…soon   but not yet
and a love that happens once
once only   just once
took my breath away
for the poet who lamented Lorca;

I now mourn for you, Leo

54

III.

Second time: a father
I'm estranged from gone in
suddenly forever, surprise
tears burning like hell...

> *you look up from your death suprised, too...*
> *no, astonished...now*
> *right now?*

No final words...
so this is what regret means...

You prowled the earth
to find some undetected hole
an escape hatch from this damned mortality
well, did you?
                find it?

So sure once I knew   bragging atheist,
not now: not out of other conviction
but simple need:

"Oh, call back," you cried

> *call back...call back...*

IV.

Put to your test
I passed; failed by doing so...
Who knew what fears of loss
insecurities from your abused "lost mother boyhood"
robbed your voice;
good, you said at first, proud
then silence   books I sent you
my readings   ignored, unattended...
The hurt that insides anger;

I lashed back   same silence once
bewildered an old Russian man, my father,
no memory of saying Kaddish
for a living daughter, for me
who couldn't ever please him
turned to a forbidden Irish enemy
and *no daughter of mine*
chased me to his bedside years later

silent.   Cold winter Maine silence
you knew it well...


Crossed my own America
met wild crazy poets with on the road imaginations
I ran with for a time for the fun the experience
beautiful souls whose spirits were their real poems
lives they would not compromise for the work
as you never compromised on the page;

I wasn't fooled   you were.

56

## V.

Infuriates me now just to think of it,
why did you have to be so impossible
forcing me to leave...
*crotchety* some said, *always complaining*
prizes that should have been yours
gone to others....yes......**should have**
I should have smashed through
to thank you for daring to be
the poet you are   a loner   scornful of the mediocrity
you threatened   to know what it cost you;

...for coming into my life
giving me yourself in your poems:
"for Linda who knows the price involved"
you wrote   certain
I knew   and would pay it...
To have that belief in me
when I didn't have it yet in myself
is gift beyond imagining...

To be the best I could
be what you asked of me,
I had to go my own way
for that I am sorry...so sorry
there are no words and words are all I have.

To say it didn't have to be this way,
you dying   or even close
so faced with it
I'd come to you in a breathless rush and...
...and how much of that
 would you believe?
                               or I ?

57

VI.

Three weeks ago   was it just three
the toilet spit out sewage
flooding my apartment
and desperate to clean up
threw out a folder with
reviews   publicity items you sent me
sat on the living room floor
tearing up a photo I took of you...

so clearly   I hear you now
calling back   ahead:

    "He was right and she was right."

––––––––––

The sound of your death is so loud, Leo,
its shadow falls across my desk
as I sit here writing in these pre dawn days
weeks that follow...
so loud

can you hear it?
Can you?

CITY GIRL

Poems by
Linda Lerner

# This Was the Year

Love yanked me up
from my father's death;
this year I shelved my hatred
like ancestral linen,
and gave up mourning
a father I never had.

I sprang out of my head
into zombie haunted streets,
dodging computerized lives,
irrelevant bodies,
a year a man and I spent
tasting each other with our eyes,
tonguing words.

Vendors shouted ice cream and hotdogs
down my ears, Koreans gorged me
with fresh anything;
I let the sun go mad
as a rabid dog on my fair skin,
and not once heard
my mother's warning voice.

I reached out to love
with more imagination, more woman
than someone knew what to do with,
the year
the present moment is fast ripening
in this first June sun.

# You Listened, Remember?

We were doing illegal in
Beatle scream time
to protest
   'he'll get you,'
     depression parents fears,
      God/father vigilante threat

for hungering: more
than housewife survival
a pensioned afterlife
we sucked the juice of taboos,
fruit in your mouth words
you couldn't get enough

Louise, peeping into a country
of weaponed men hot
knives in their pants,

you listened, into invisibility
slow violation, listened…

Us staggering high headed
out of East Village railroad
all night riding him
still roughhousing
in our blood

your heart beating cries
Louise, remember?  Girl who
never kicked fright aside
nobody's moll,

we all risked.
Come to us now
as if we
could get them rocking
out of Liverpool on

Sullivan again and
you'd be burning green
Wallenda woman.

# Risking

Death swoops down
snatching dancer from
hell of sweeping up newspapers
he once split across
country headlining...

Who does not feel for him?
Our child hearts break...
Aren't enough prayers,
tears in all the churches;

but voices accuse
unnatural...and a
man past hot youth's
blood craving

risking his life for
vampire kissed fate.

Puritan us, liberated
Cowers, green in
secret lusts...

Romantic horror stirs
wets our brillowed insides
we can barely grasp...
scares us alive.

# First Ride

Sneaking out of
father's threats to
back seat car ride
with boy 'not of her kind'
was going somewhere
in wild haired America,
but in and out so fast...

Sometimes on a night beach
shell sand needling skin,
seaweed stink and
he sunbasked blind;

no talk
reefer filling hours,
no talk where he was
why she couldn't come;

must have seen,
crumpled, fist-eyed,
even with back to her
seen—

illegal weekend with
girl 'out of his church'
would never marry
and she only
wanted initiation;

love, was love
at first, didn't want
licensed anything…love
but how many times
can a man…

"Like medicine," he said
in the back seat
dark of youth.

# Regrets Some Women Have

At not-quite-forty, they have
a tantrum of regrets:
homeless motorcycle-driven years
through pension plans, around
housing lists, past dark-suited men
with clock-setting habits,
to adventure naked out of sleep,
to bite into anything hot & spicy;

at not-quite-forty, they start
insuring themselves
against mortality, children & medical plans,
a car race into whitewashed marriages
and dull jobs with fine-print protection
against a geography of disasters.

It's sprouts & wheat germ
and out of the sun & summers
of hot tasting smells;
it's fat men with memo pads,
carrot juice martinis & exercise classes,

a frenzied 'no time for regret' ride
with old wildness and
no time, the taste of sawdust lips
& dry tongues, healthy lives
that don't quench, & no time,
worse regrets, and
no time   no time.

## All Us Casualties

I.

Westchester Bernice back
from unlicensed honeymoon

                slums through
women taking it in Greenwich Village
walkthrough dark talk.

Was the time
pill popped freedom in
first bar hopping woman
long haired men licked
off last milk rings of virginity.
Old shame reversed.

Bernice of Westchester never left,
white gowned heart
stood up at invisible altar
after he came...plunging nights
waiting...

                What friend Jane
drank through jazz night men
blind to get...

Once a man
she lay beside like
good Annie doll nobody
told it's all right to move
fondled her, never anything
more, one night asked her
to take it like a lollipop.
Felt she did something wrong.

II.

Jane on way to stage fame
listened to Doc Cheatham
trumpet God out of heaven
at Sweet Basil, like
she was alone, every


cell of her skin jumping;
whole place pulsed hot
for her.

Got to Bernice, too.
A woman's yearning
felt a man's...

in the tight skin of excuse
she left with nothing
feeling like she had
gotten something.

Fleas bite hadn't become
needle's sting, no death
threat load to down;

                    OD'd on freedom,
women hid 'till death do us part' love wish
like old big belly sin
and sang in the wake of our lives
picked flowers and sang.

III.

Bernice, fifteen years out of
Westchester never left
ready but

death plaguing undercover in
our greed, already
had us. Victims
killers now. Too.

Imagine, what she once feared,
now craves....should
for her life fear.
A life cheated of life.

Death at her heels
Jane, driven by addiction...habit-
fixed too many years...late

bar stool nights
risk she'll go home
with anyone, every night risk...

heart beating quick
like when she was girl.

# City Rain

For days, rain blasting away
and nothing
on the bare trees,
nothing
on faces pinched out of Burberrys and London Fogs,
but the shadows of trees
branching dead bark everywhere
and someone's rage
at an umbrella turned inside out.

NO-ONE'S-PEOPLE

Linda Lerner

# I Said No

To my piped clogged apartment
the plumber comes without tools...
"they've taken them!"
Irish brogue anger swears
he'll get even...

      A robbed immigrant's voice.
      Your voice, father, in my home
      you never visited.

Deep in tenement Brooklyn near
streets scarred by trolley tracks
I lusted after my "forever" world
an artist's, not yours, father.

Need for love insatiable need...
Manhattan promised exchange currency.
10 cent subway treat brought
more than magical river/
bridge out of a poverty childhood.

Wasn't street crime/hunger I
feared then, the inside cold.
Robbed yourself, what could you give me?

Forced out of your father's house
barely fourteen, never saw Russia again.
A boy exiled for his own good,

over his brothers chosen
you never forgave survived
a foreign depression
guilt ridden...never forgot.

Hungry America of your youth now
corners high rent streets with paper cups...
A blond Mayflower dirtied ghost child
no business being there
embarrasses us, we walk quickly past...
collapsed pushcarts blanket the
lower East/upper West sides,
dark-skinned men and women not
pale East Europeans: same hunger. Yours.

That awful summer after the car accident
you blamed me for, my leg in a cast
I lay helpless: you screamed
needle jabbing fear into my brain
nearly killed me....
only nine, I knew
something more than a father's love
a fear of eviction raged
in the skin of your soul:
a god praising anger
you couldn't put into words...

Nine years old and I knew
when you looked at me, Jane,
there was no Jane.

I was you, the heaven
you slaved for
as you were for your father.

            And I said NO.
            Quick as a sniper's shot
            NO for my life.

Denied the freedom you fought
risked life for   NO   hitting me
with its tire wheels in
the air   NO   through thick apartment
walls no one penetrates

Used my Irish lover like a weapon,
got you to say
the Jewish prayer for the dead
for me, so angry like I
tricked you into doing it...

In the lies subtracting years
cheating myself   NO   to
children sucking the breath out of me
waking sleep years I can't remember.
Hunger for love that
made me anyone's prey
kept me in strait jacket fear
he'd be you.
Hole in the middle of my life.

O father, understanding is
not forgiveness.  Something...yes.
We robbed each other
doing to ourselves what was done.

When you died I mourned
the father you stole from me,
a boy exiled for his own survival:
I mourned a child
no father told he loved.
Not you.  I never mourned for you.

I will not do so now.
From the other side of the
bridge I'm slowly crossing,
I will not do so.

# First Kind of Love

Just two scared kids
hitchhiking in the '60s skies.
The boy ignoring her for the stewardess
his church choir blue eyes could con.
    "yes...been there before; often."

The girl, a Russian immigrant's daughter,
the whole flight imagining a crash
never looked up from a Graham Greene novel;
prayed to a god she killed.

A week later, up from a tequila night
in Mexico City, they jumped on a moving bus to Acapulco.

Wrapped in an Indian blanket
along a cliff's edge in the sombrero dark
came with every thrust and jolt:
The astonishment of themselves.

Never feared it would go over.
And it never did.

# Fast Horse Riding

This was fast horse riding
through unknown dark;
rein scarred hands clutched
excitement/delicious fear

                that night

we rode to a place defined
by motion, body on body
to a cliff's edge...

Pause like a pomegranate
burned in the air.
We didn't dare touch
feared to break open;
we regressed down.  And again.
Wore the night out
speeding to dismantle the
mortality of us.

# City Walking Song

1.

Through market place streets
vendors and homeless voices pushing
                    past
someone's exploded need
                    they keep walking
shoulders and backs harnessed with bulging canvas:
end of a century, immunity too broken down
          jean-patched sexless
          they shove into sidewalk bins, crowded
solitude of cafe/night shelters.
A studio room costs
                    must keep moving.
Twenty-four hours bought and sold.
                    sometimes

2.

someone grabs an orange
from a too open market, and
                    a herd of west-
sides kick up untamed prairie wilderness
hard riding pursuit through earth
paved for civilization.
                    A cowboy
in sports tweeds jumps
                    into a knife plunge
and everyone feels better. Real or imagined:
taste of blood on city hands.
                    And keep walking

3.

around work hours
                    through tunneled weekends....
videos flickering out of business books,
cars with no radio/no money windows
along 8th street Broadway
like a river floating
                    up
steep flights, peeling off wall gray
into studios to sweat death out.

Skin nylon-tight on muscle/bone
bodies not meant to arouse;
in every leap
                    the blood scream joy:
                         safe flight.

4.

on the road people
who never leave the city

fear the green quiet
locked up night town's solitary
                              move
like packs of lost nomads
through youth marching

against war and illness
against cutbacks: blamed on
a governor or president.

The whole city charged
with rage marching
out of sleep-scared
cannot stop
            marching.

## No-One's-People

Men down to their last skins
headed toward shelter on Wards Island.
Made ghosts by the fog cold, not human, no
it was all right....teens wolfed through.

                  Huddled hunger

trapped on footbridge had no money
he couldn't understand, trick
or...? No-one's-people
gave all hallows permission to
witched boys, Zulu and Dracula faced

                        ...had no watch
                        gloves, "jump" they
                          screamed, "jump..."

Lured by fires once kindled to
ward off evil, powered with bats, knives

                    all he had was  NO

they ravaged the island;
boys who cindered a dog's tail
tasted its sweet pleasure now
played with ritual excuse.

Words like vultures
he wouldn't/threatened to
skin life, couldn't
make him....

Death headlined next morning.

Outside the island of their muscled minds
        NO   raised its heart
                beating fist.

# Sixty

All night a voice out of
smoky alehouses
told me he was sixty,
sweaty voice from love
sagging on rusty springs
creaking poverty's music
across America laid
down his life…
6…0 he said as though
he couldn't grasp the
sudden wound ripping
flesh sense of it.
His rock gray eyes never
budged from where I sat;
all night in boozy dark
he clutched a woman's
last fling of youth
like a tourniquet
and wooed her girl-heart.

*This book is dedicated to the memory of my parents, Frieda &*
*Philip Lerner and for Andrew Gettler who gave me second birth.*

1996

from *She's Back*

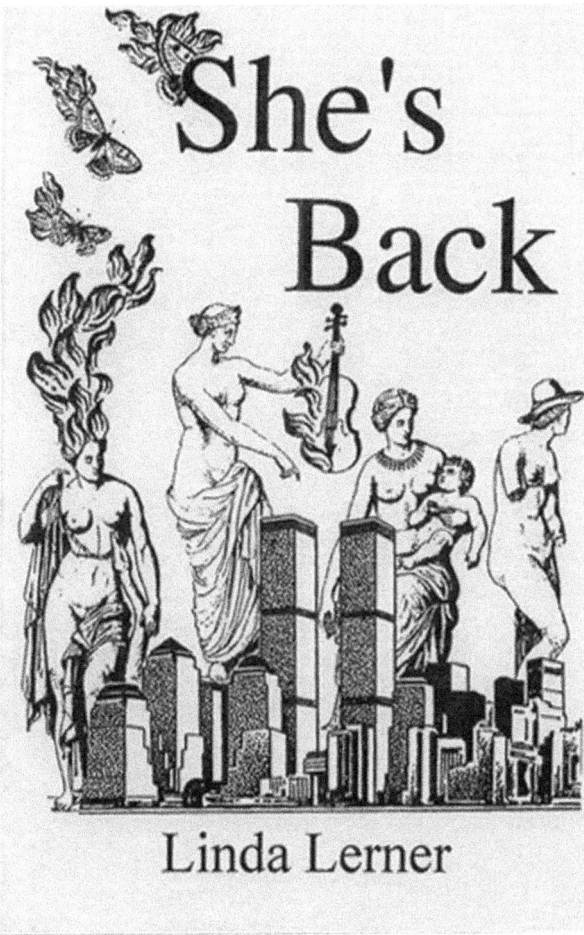

# She's Back

## Linda Lerner

# I Said Yes

...Left New York terminal
where hunger sharpens its blade;
I gave not to feel
someone's pain rip my throat,
to get my life back.

Boston: city trapped with marbleized
struggles for freedom;
learned memories of rebellion.

I came for the poetry
a soul's hunger miked
in bars, park;

came to be with him.
My father's outlaw daughter again.

I heard his Kaddish in the nerves
of my womanhood, and could not
lift its stone weight;
no man's woman, I slammed
my body shut in full yearning.

And in the noose of freedom
ran...sometimes hugged blankets
in dark solitary my arms nearly
crushing my ribs...sometimes
with a man's lust inside
I ran praying, *catch me*, to anyone.
Escaped a father's persecution.
Not his curse.

Now in room 128 Lord Wakefield Motel
not far from Bullet House and
revolutionary battle bridge
no longer young, in
the grip of a lover's arms
the Irish of my father's other rage

I tasted the words in his eyes
when he asked
felt the soft skin
of his hard maleness

speak to this woman;
mattered more than all that history...
and with every rebellious cell of me
yes, for the first time   yes

# She's Back

She's tasting a boy's first
wet appetite, like the girl
she once was

             strutting on
a tenement firescape
in the protection of marital wars;

On a rock blast of Elvis
swings into a blacklisted country.

Busy with bread-in-the mouth arithmetic
parents, depression era refugees
they saw only poverty.

A man old enough to
be that girl's father
now holds my hand past
the pretense of skin

kisses a woman's mind out of lips
in a Greenwich Village bar
smack into another boro/home,
                    and she,
drum pulse in every cell, she's
giving him a girl's new body.

As though a heavy booted wish
stomped out years...pact
against her womanhood.
She made against her mother's slavery.

   Before she knew
the price of that murder.

# Knowing the Difference

After making love
temperature plunges, heart
beats us to edge of something;
we hold tight: embryonic.
Come clean, we
enter differently now
touch past gender.
You might say all reason.
Against what drove us here
to what we'll make:
let go.

# What's All This Jazz?

Coming late to sex and jazz,
taking nothing for granted/taking everything...

unbuttoning/unzipping is
the cry of trumpets, growl of sax;
in her tossed underwear, the clarinet's wail.

Improvising out of solitude,
there are no wrong movements.
The man she faces, the man making all
this possible, hitting those spots

maybe doesn't hear the sound of her movements;
just wants to get off
before dinner/after work, if
there was any work, maybe hears
a car horn or sanitation truck...

doesn't know about her unexpected gig,
who she's jamming with in the dark.
Or really care.  He's tired, hungry.

But this is her night.  Her turn.
Whole body jumping, a '40s jazz joint
she's never been in.

# Graveside

One week before the unveiling,
September rust weather;
I followed my mother,
sentences like blind roads:
"Come, I kept calling him
from the kitchen,
the chicken is done,
every day...
                now..."
Her eyes cameoed
a husband of forty years,
"Someplace far.  Like Russia."
A winter cold worrying in her voice.

"It's easier without the fighting.
Quieter since December...
At the center
a man proposed, old,
needs taking care of,"
she said straightening herself
a young girl's way.
"Others too."
She looked at me,
snow in her eyes.

"I never came with him.
He knew, said one night afterwards,
'it's all right if you want to,
with someone else.'
You were fifteen, maybe sixteen,"
she said, before I asked.

"I'm too old for a man now,
but once it would be nice to know..."
Her voice reached past itself.
You understand?"

# The Last Visit

*for my father, Philip Lerner 4/15/1900–12/30/1985*

Somebody's father is sick,
Tubes sprout from his mouth, his arms...
The cold/white of winter
borrowing human form.
He looks at me,
those same damn hazel eyes.

And my father,
in the shape of his anger,
my father, fist clenched,
eyes blazing in the old way,
rises, and once more, thunders
toward me, the daughter
whose death he mourned three times:
I was nine, I didn't know
of any passage, first, through grief,
just his anger/blame, fast speeding
like that car...
It struck me,
all that terrible summer,
my foot in a cast...it struck me...
I lay in bed, I listened,
and years later
in the arms of my Irish lover,
his voice, the Jewish prayer for the dead,
and when I left his house, unmarried,
"No daughter of mine/no daughter of mine!"

A nurse taps my shoulder.
It is over.  Visiting hours.
An old Russian man holds out
his hand.  I take it.
After all, what does he have to do
with any father/daughter tug of war
in my memory.  I let go.
I think of kissing his cheek.

# Price on Our Heads

Yesterday the World Trade Center was bombed.
Arabs.  My father's enemy.
"I told you so" warnings
drag me down…
My lover never met
but knows in his Jewish gut,
smells his vodka breath,
under six feet of earth
sniffs out "Irish"
                shakes this foundation.

I think of that bigger blast;
fanatics from a world we buried…
destruction of innocence as great as lives.

Who said there is such a thing as death?
                Only bodies vanish.
Nobody who ever lived
leaves this earth.

# The Price of an Apple

The good days
are the days I worry
about the price of an apple,
and how much lettuce costs.

I calculate
when the fare will be $2.00 a ride,
my rent $1,000 a month;
no money for the dentist,
I worry about what man
will make love to a toothless woman.

I forget how long
since I licked off a kiss,
or how often love ends in mourning.

After work I go
and forget the hunger
food can't satisfy,
even love, the hunger
that drives me to write page
after page for the unborn,
to write against the stopped heart,
write against loneliness, against aging.

# Old People at the Bank

Pre war Europe
crumbles in their voices;
their eyes are homeless.

A few decades back
this could have been a breadline,
ousted Russian nobility,
skin like thread-worn silk.

But, this is a bank,
the hardcore '80s:
Several accounts per person,
interest compounded—
we see a membrane of lies.

The line lengthens like an argument.
Dark suits sway back and forth
with obscene urgency.

The old people look away.
Their business isn't done.
It spans an ocean,

severed ties like birth cords,
a lifetime of gains and losses to compute.
They will not be rushed.

Bravo, I want to say.
It takes enormous courage
to get this needy,
to stand on this line.

# Played Jazz Violin Like an Out of Town Junkie

He played down to nerve
 twisting himself in sound;
played from his gut; dead screams
   rumbling underground
              speared into trees;

he played to free himself,
played with the soul of his mind
         of his flesh,
in the sweltering night
              licking ice cream crowd
he played like he had no time left
like a junkie, using his bow like his sex;
       the Man supplying his own fix.
Arching, hips forward
            desire without object
he curved high around each note;
       hitting bottom
played like he had no skin;
like no cool New Yorker ever would.

# Mugging

They've come from defiling a mall;
it's Friday before
snorting, big radio blast
with girls...youths
teased by shop windows
stirring urges they out price

now feast on new
credit card wealth.
Block is quiet.

She looks easy;
"Victim" rings fast cash
through minds that
see but don't see;
need for love makes her
someone else's fragile victim.

Cry pulled like a
knife startles the terror
of kids out of them.

A man turning the corner
happens so fast she
wonders if something masculine
really grabbed, tried to
force her down...
"You're all right" he
says without stopping
ever intending to

and they're running in
screaming daylight back to
summer job only job
dealing their life for life.

# Going Down

it was all sea
crowd of fish hunger,
slurping…wrapped
in your pleasure
dark of new visibility
I saw with taste buds of flesh.
Salt/wind licked
sun roared through bedroom night.
Felt like something coming born.

        seemed hours
before you surfaced
centuries older.  I hauled
you into my arms; glimpsed the
imprint of a sea's earth
mapped on your face
barred from my
curious woman's eyes.
…now beached ashore,
your hair streaming
barely breath to speak
a man's other need
before I dove in.

# Protest

A door gunner in Vietnam
was flying toward a
woman he never met

brought up to fear
men who spoke with
their bodies; above all, flying.

        ...To California,
the lie of discharge papers.
Shooting up was shooting to kill.
nobody gets out of war
that easily.

Grew up in range of marital fire
surprise ambush attack,
she knew about war,
friendly fire;

        destroyed
for just being there, being you,
what they feared to be...just being.

Closer now.   Still flying.
He escaped the enemy again.
Thought she did too

protesting war, shoplifting
in wild-talk cafes,
gypsy artist winged high
into third world country,
someone beside her
she thought was him.

Men's eyes slipped into her skin
across a room, kept them
by keeping distance.

In the tight bandanna of freedom
lived the life she wasn't ready for;
returned with stories.
Happened but didn't.

Once knew girls like her,
had all the answers. Taught him
the breathing of love…one did.
Noise of death made him forget.

Took cover in geographyless routines:
business ascent, the business
of marriage. Wake sleep skies
couldn't see where he was going
kept flying…level disturbance.

To find her
he had to become
her perception of him.

She dreamed of him who
would find her
where others failed;
slept off the solitude.

On a flight he couldn't afford,
knapsack of tales to prove it,
crash landed.

Mistress of lies still;
what did it matter.

In his vision of her
        became
what she pretended to be.

Created each other;
made love like it was
the beginning of the world.

So it is.

# A Ghost's Progeny

He protests limits; like me
if I were still
guaranteed *forever*,
knocking about in '60s male permission,
instead of planning a life with his father:

His son's mortality mapped all
over his face. Arrogance falters.
I am only the woman who loves him.
He is only the boy's father

following him in the valley of
the shadow of himself—1968:
survives napalm, fire bombings, seeing
the wounded, dead helicoptered out;
      survives his own death.
      To tell of others.
1993: new threats camouflage Nam's
      old terrors.

Not airborne over mined jungle
      like his father
but in mother country, promised
protection of his birth home, faces
the Judas of his own lust. Maybe

he too will be lucky,
carrying in his blood, his ribs,
the seeds of survival history:
living his own life. And another's.

# Une Maladie Cruelle

The first time I saw him defect
    from mortality
tights skinned on rock muscle
he split past gender and country.
The theater heated like an oven.

I was trying for womanhood,
some boy always poking....
One who played my mute body
listened when I told him,
surely must have heard
a sudden musicality of movements
he couldn't take credit for.
I feel sorry for him now,
and that girl looking up with impossible desire.

A long time since
that impoverished evening
I ate jelly sauced spaghetti
in a borrowed apartment
with a boy aching toward manhood

and spoke of that dancer.
Never any less.
Even when he must have been.
One night, too close,
I nearly saw his arms fail
his ballerina
and go unacknowledged.
The way it is with lovemaking,
his body was his mind.

Another night, wrapped in the
fleshed thoughts of a man's love,
news of a God's mortality was aired.

# Electricity

To transmit current
through fingers, tongue
lips, watch you grow big

    my god, what it does
    to this woman

you now enter: one pleasure
balances against the other.

So long in death's region
I lived past its comprehension.

Then, by Braille touch
of accident, found

this measure of current.
Shoots through flesh of mind
and breath; all my words.
Makes poems for you.

# Come Close to Perfect

*from Andrew Gettler's poem "how much is enough?"*

In Odessa...stuffed cabbage country
of exiles, hand-me-down
revolution talk

    brown coal eyes warmed
    the skin off...

horse backed police
sticking it to huddled
need in Thompkins Square Park

    burned brown coal...
    warmth spread/wet.

June night heated;
couldn't shake decades of
into bone cold.

After being alone
a long time homeless

happiness comes like an
eviction notice

shocks like dive into
heart stopped cold waters
revives so quick,
one is the other.

After being hungry so long
the heart is belly full.
Starved clean of fight.

Three months/never
feared it would end.
Dreaded it would not.

# New & Selected Poems

## Linda Lerner

## For Survival

                    I've seen him
blast thru all the bullshit
words capsule; over coffee
leave someone stranded on
                    fissured terrain
when he swung into
a mental bureaucracy of excuse
and staggered off...
                    Several times a year
cut up   naked   hands me
his mind on a platter.
                    We smash the walls
love creates, undress
politeness: perform
                    love's dangerous work.

## That Other Couple

**1.**

Something said accidentally torpedoes...
he's back in Nam trying to save
men dead for twenty years;
she's a child in family hell
and they're running for cover
disrupting us again, we who have
nothing to do with them now.

The woman vanishes but doesn't leave.
he gets angry.  She too.
There's plenty of alcohol,
betrayals that go back before they met:
the girl a father murdered who
lives on;
a boy's remembrance
of unpermitted love.

We hear them thru walls we make up:
two people pilfering from each other
love freely given.
We wonder if it's possible to
move far enough away...
we who must pull them out from
the wreckage afterwards;
pray for a beating heart.

**2.**

And they're here too, young enough
to be our children. If we had them.
Angry youth back from some war....
Reared on Catholicism's threats and
Beat absolution, wants to be

the father he didn't have.
Means there's kids, or will be,
but his artist girl rejects
her mother's shackles.  We be
his daughter and his wife.

Noise of silent conflict no word
arguments threaten our fantasies.
And we wonder if our lives would be
any better now, had we met them
                    years before.

We who only have each other
hold our breath "yes" when
she rubs his back one night
seeding the urge to bear his child.

Past deciding, it is easy to make
that decision now; see them
lie down together as if
no wrong had ever been committed.

Like that night she rubbed his back
unknotting someone else's work.
And her mind just let go.

## Legacy

Sunday rains blues
      all day rains…
Her chilling voice in your joints,
making you hard again;
twisted into a mother's misshapen need
your hands speak love
with difficulty now.
Smash walls to
hurt what isn't you.
        get out the rage.
Knuckles bulge/unforgiving.
Wind swirling rain twists
      love's intention
continues her work; so
nothing ever turns out right.
Want to warn your woman
of a man's harm/not you,
to keep her safe, but
it takes quite a few these days
      to drown him,
get up the courage…
              You
keep smashing walls
and the rain…all day rain
won't let you stay soft for long;
wails louder than ever inside.

## Blues Song

Must have cost plenty for one man
to take this subway ride,
startled by a buddy from another life
slouching in downtown fringed
leather duds across the aisle,

                hard even
with two kids tugging his shoulder,
every minute whining, "is this the stop,"
to forget how it once was...
                    urges older than they
in those "ready to go" eyes...
Saw the bagged signature of permission;
taste memory did the rest.

Words trampled in dirty noise
didn't hurt up beat jazz the
other blew without a horn,
blew the whole ride, improvising
                on the sound just
long enough to hand that
man's boy a single bill
when their stop came, give him
that spoken look kids know from home.

# Jamming with the Angels—Town Hall & Elsewhere

*(5/19/94)—for Andrew*

A four day beat revival
of your own to mark  50
your day
       happening
            to be theirs
          took us
to Town Hall/wake-
ning of Jack's spirit
in shirt & tie   worn pals
squeezing into old jive sounds
                in you burst
thru twenty year restraints/
             ordering of days…
always had an edge, though,
            never quite fit
suit you wore
ripped off at last, as
Allen once might have done.
With a swinging chick
you stumbled on in me
         one night
blasted on jazz    on wine on sex
high on you
         hit a road
swerved off in reckless youth;
four days   warned anyone who'd listen
         of a second coming.
(not bad for a mortal)
candle lit   you blew
all the Pall Mall burnt
stale air you could cough up
             blew   half century
              rebellion
                into
                 orbit

# Old West Tale

*"Let's be the angels of the world's desire and take the world to*
*bed with us before we die. "* —*Allen Ginsberg*

When Allen conjured up a
green motor-horse for Neil,
two hotshot heroes high
     on beer and vision
riding over the Rockies down
the Plains of America
he cracked open myth:
behind barbed wire technology,
beneath asphalt progress...
          what
was closed for decades
     in this woman
till someone saw it
was there, yes
untouched, unspoiled...
          what
forgotten Lusk, Wyoming
did when it lassoed the future
with fiber optics stirring
     old western promise
yes     in mid century
        mid life
inventing trails to discover;
and took me to New Mexico
and keeps urging me west...
     California, Arizona
to Denver...to Denver....
And if there was no horse
no sand-wind biting flesh
     in that poet's frontier,
just engine breath and
look out from a green jalopy window

sent him soaring…
if there was
no more permanence than
a few years thefted magic and
fast riding with my lover
in a Brooklyn apartment
brought us to a miraculous
never before beheld
as we were
as we could be again:
in the youth of imagination.

# Men Called Jack

*for Jack Micheline poet on the front line*

*"The eye is connected to the heart"*
—*Micheline*

across San Francisco/America
single room occupancy lives refusing to learn "the lord is
my shepherd"/unable
escapees from the Bronx
without teeth   failing eyesight
earth crusted nails
soap can't remove
proud of it
dangerous men breathing poems....

> *isn't just words/eyes talk*
> *way you move your hand*
> *turn your head*
> *gives a poet away...*

men called Jack
nurturing more
than flesh and bone
flesh and bone of
what matters
child-eyes pushing 70 years
scrawled on brown bags/forgotten
yellowing pages   stuffed
boxes scaling
peeling walls to some heaven

outlaws/madmen fighting
what straitjackets imagination
refusing to be herded
to green pastures

return its soul to America
   and damned for it
men called Jack/colorists
painting red and
purple and green
murals on dullness
scaring the shit
out of
"lord is my shepherd"
              America

## What I Miss *(Oh, to be naked again!)*

I miss being naked with someone,
the clothes-on-lie nobody believed;
tried not to see
        what they saw
        down jackets couldn't conceal
as we walked along Montague street
             below zero cold...

I miss being the same woman
whose breasts, cunt were hidden
as when they weren't,
            sometimes
did my thinking; knew
      it was my mind
      made me desirable.

I miss fighting for space:
      in bed, at my desk...
that presence I flexed my will against,
          comforted to feel,

miss being not free
to stay out all night,
      no explanations...
to get on a bus going anywhere
         not return;
leave my life, if I chose: no guilt.
        Freedom fought for
        not against.

I miss someone hearing my thoughts
         before I have words...
refusing to let me get away
with what others permitted him;
miss being a shrine at the
mouth of someone's worship:
                              enslaved.


...someone to love
bad boy of a mother's worry
a woman's arousal: my "wayward knight."


I miss feeling beautiful...
on a day when I'm sick,
upset, know a stranger wouldn't
                              even notice,
more beautiful than anyone I know,
beautiful as on that hot June night
                      his eyes
found my nakedness; wouldn't release it.


I miss being someone's baby
his incestuous love, jailbait
                      secret;


someone to run-a-way with,
cross the borders of this AIDS
infected, social police state
to illegal '60s country...
I miss being screaming naked
beyond pride; anything.

         US: I miss us

ANYTIME BLUES

poems by

**LINDA LERNER**

Wayne Hogan

*For Tony*

*Brought together by one who*
*had   IT   absolutely*
*made sure I got   IT*
*Yeah   "a joyful noise…"*

*We keep   IT   alive*

*"The journey is only from there to there to there."*
*—Anonymous Bronx Sage*

*"Slowly I Realized*
*The Best Way To*
*Hold on,*
*Was to just*
*let go."*

*(Graffiti found—from* 24.7 Artzine)

# Blizzard '96

saw a man talking to a pigeon
in front of blimpies
over 20 inches of snow fallen
he looks the pigeon straight in the eye,

  "you & me got a problem,"

gray stubble on bloated reddish skin
dirty cup of coffee in his hand
and deep in record-breaking pristine white
    softening new york harshness...

  "where we gonna get us some food?"

fairytalecity no cars trucks
people acting so nice
and this man nobody sees
  want to tell him
i know about hunger-worry too
    but how

on a full stomach
able to buy all the food i want
tell him how difficult it is
to find a few seeds
my man gone to some bottom
vanished like all the seeds
    how to
make my voice heard
 thru all this snow

## What Do I See When I See

Old man stares into his cup of black coffee,
black even after he drinks it;
                      see him
in McDonald's window, well dressed
crouching in his trench hole-dark
                          late afternoons
on Court street
                    on my way to/this detour
                              then
back to old turf: hunting
for job/apartment, life in rougher
                      '90s climate/
whining from bones/joints...
Odd time for love to crocus;
                    feel
urge to hit the sky-road
ignore the economics of breathing...
                    see
backpacking angels taking flight,
no planes, miles in the air
smoking cigarettes, having drinks
thumbing their noses at everyone
more frightened of unemployment than death
                           who
don't see that old man
              never will
perfect flying weather, and...

    *Hey lady, watch where*
    *you're going...*

>           Big Mac/breaks
> inches from me…blinding gasoline sun,
> angry 5 o'clock stampede; horns jazz
>                         murder improv,
> someone's shoe nipping my heel
> screams, "bitch, watch where…"
>
> And I don't know where
>                         on Court Street
>                         March, 1995

## When an Editor Praising My Poems Asks *but why* & Do You Have Any That *are more*

what can I tell her
this is New York not Oregon
my metrocard only takes me
so far   most of it underground:
Brooklyn   Manhattan   Bronx/
thru conductor's
announcements of police action
meeting people so programmed
they don't even know
kids warring up for the day
pushing: death   god   music
off track rhythms
my poems pick up &
grab an editor out west
if only i'd discard
the   *bummed out...dead lives...*
the   *desolation*
couldn't see the rhythm
is the sound of the image &
can't be separated
as I from this city...
                    underground
where I choose to live
my poems are born
& real is a pain
in the butt   nagging me
for spare anything   my
space...REAL

underground because
sometimes a guy pulls out
a horn & blows
on a street in blazing sun
he's underground blowing
& it's that sunflower
Ginsberg saw by some dirty railroad tracks
full of a city's *industrial grime*
*golden inside*
unmistakable/
sunflower

# I Don't Always Anything

I know a lot of dead people.
         one PhD'd brain/
dead someone, scholars books;
does/says what her programmed
mind allows.  On impact
classifies, categorizes...
                         inherited.
Enough to secure herself
         out of breath.
Knows a lot.  Not that.
When necessary, I seek her out.
Feels like jumping bail to hear

         *but you always...*
         *and, yesterday*

Friend, yesterday I wasn't even born:
         in this living space
         this heart, this thought.
Her good wishes, killer
threat alerts my survival instinct:
I reach for outrageous
she hasn't seen/heard...
Ah, but she's good;
         a minute, and

*you're a poet, that explains....*

# Farewell to a Downdrodden Saint

*2/27/98*

don't much like this age
hankering after puritan taboos
holy/holier than thou
about everything
hail and brimstone Cotton Mathers
running my city, country
anything alive, x-rated
holy art not exempt either...

walk down any street and see
people huddled in doorways sneaking
a drag, scared criminal by
new morality: in the name of health, family
someone killed, a building blown up;
doesn't matter what we call it now...

nabbed for jay walking
refusing to keep within the lines
overstepping like a child who
doesn't see a line
crayoned red over a coloring book picture
and called into the principal's office
to explain what i couldn't
can't still...breathe between lines
i don't see:   *do not step*
*on the grass   dance on the grass*
like a child doesn't know
how to put herself in
a prison, child with young
or old skin who knows in
the scheme of things/no scheme:

133

refusing today to join the huffing pack
chasing down the POET'S death
with their writing tools,
i've taken this crazy detour,
will not even write his name
      in defiance
      in deference

i bump into the POET
seated in a crummy luncheonette
in my poem, coffee and a bagel
with a smear of cream cheese
out of his Bronx boyhood,
that old floppy hat he wore in
San Francisco, day i met him
and we spent together;

bumming a cigarette, he winks at me
smiling flowers and children
all over my poem
wherever he sees gray,
making a toast:
      to life
      to life

# Bluespoet

*for Tony Moffeit (who never writes on black ice)*

bluespoet is riding
in his car riding the sound
of the road   of a jazz horn
the pen riding urges
in his blood his genes
riding blind with sight
down colorado mountains
            riding his vision
thru boundary semantic
            of living & dead
riding the umbilical cord
            back to his mother
            to the ghost of himself
riding his own death
frees himself of it
            on a mountain pass
in colorado his car spinning
on black ice on a word
                        a line
            spinning
                        off
            anytimeblues
into a ravine
song
drumming
life back
bluespoet must ride to breathe
cup up bleeding
bluespoet gets back in the car
to saddle america
tapping secret energies
of the earth heals himself
miles of mississippi delta

backroads   and always margarita
in the rain & snow
margarita filling his head
crazy rhythms   driving his pen
across the sangre de cristo mountains
        into mystery & danger

riding a train's whistle
wolf howl moan of a voodoo woman
riding a love supreme

to new orleans
bluespoet is riding
        he's riding

        OUT

the breath

# Because You Can't   I Will

write the poem about all the nannies
in this Brooklyn neighborhood we
lived in   mine   not yours
the hood missing   Bronx edge
you grew up in
raised three kids
*made-it*-relief   after each
wiping plenty of ass   sometimes
punching fists thru walls
to get thru…
Vietnam   marriage   jobs…
cleaned up your own shit

no wonder you were so struck
by these nannies   walked
uneasily thru this safe zone
looking over your shoulder
quick draw eyes on the ready/
feared losing that edge
becoming too sure…

this is the poem you walked away from
the woman who wanted you to stop smoking
drawn to your Pall Mall breath
to give up:   the
spirit that flew you to her
and took you away:

this is the world you couldn't afford

# Halloween 1997

the dead wake from poems
i've buried them in
calling long distance
     *how far from dementia*
i don't ask a mother
calling her teenage runaway
       not me...
risen from the kaddish
my father hit me with
for disobedience: nobody's child/

i've earned the right:

wasn't me she bathed fed
clothed sent to school
even knew
      but sounds ok...
if i had a daughter/don't
but if i did
i'd want one like her
as wild & bad
locked up with that lover
my mother imagines me with
not stuck in this Halloween dark
alone in my skin
unprotected from ghosts/

another born her month/day
returns now same week as she
     *what's happening?*

back from the jazz funeral
i gave him in blood ink
death he insisted on
pulled off once more...
ghost of a mother's misaimed need
ghost of Vietnam   of himself
poet of ghosts i wept over
& cursed   called husband:

   *what's happening?*

# A Nod to Dylan Thomas

give 'em hell, i think/hearing
that my mother socked the head
nurse trying to tie her down
when she got up to walk out
of old age's death
screamed for the police/attack dogs...
i was at a memorial
for a street singer last
of the troubadour poets
child of his spirit, among others
eulogizing a guy who raised his own hell

*against the Goddamn dead*
*...that rule this world*

i wanted to see this woman/my mother
who lived in a corner of
her life bent over an
ironing board   a stove   gave
love the only way she knew:
heated up & served
disappointed by what she got back
break free, do what she never dared
wanted her to know just as much,
i couldn't give what hadn't been given
and resented both equally now;
but when i heard what she
did in that hospital
i cheered her on:
i am child of her spirit
as much as his
socking it to death in every poem:

hey jack, it isn't only the dead
the children   too   rule

# To My Mother in a Nursing Home

i bring flowers
not poems
she called   *clutter*   of those
zines i gave her...forgotten
in her dying/
recalled now like the love
i withheld couldn't
break thru a wall to give:
or the family
she wanted for me
not her/not only for her
i bring flowers
that don't last too long
beauty that maintains itself
not poems
wrenched from the gut
brawling too loud
for her deaf ears...
to my mother who is dying
i bring flowers
not poems

# When the Holy Man Came

could have been a rock concert
        heavy metal, grunge
resurrected Elvis   Lennon
Garcia, newly dead, no one quite believed...
                        tight security, but
black garbed adoration
        crashed sexual boundaries,
                incense speeding heads
                                back....

Woodstock/Beatles' generation
screaming voice out of throat
                could have been
Rolling Stones's second coming
        Mick performing live
                miracle
sparking a crowd's orgasm.
Been an atheist long as I recall
but recognized the fervor:
When my lover looked into
my eyes when he touched and lifted me
                holy...holy...

# Poem for American's Unofficial Poet Laureate

he came to pay homage   Whitman's unnatural first born
been ill   couldn't focus   on/off with his glasses
searching for words left
in a California supermarket long ago
stumbled on now...
we held our breath
prayed he'd make it thru   yes   once more
      be who he was...

his hand weighed down by the book
i gave him to sign

      voice badgering
        *please howl*
      *i never heard you howl*
            *again   please*

*I am not a performing dog*   he howled...

      he was there for Whitman
      we for him
      a difficult evening...

in business suit   frameless glasses
could have been that rebel's father/
we kept looking for him at readings
hoped to hear   and sometimes
in that weary old man's voice
that brash kid who
went to Dr. Williams with his poems
           that legendary cry...

I never met the man   **really**   met him
too old   not old enough
for student or contemporary
heterosexual at that
I came late to what he   &   they   were about
        all the way when i did…

learned he was dying from a daily tabloid
read it on a crowded no. 5 subway:
                    right then knew
something major was going down
                with the century
        …………

                went down
next day   flashed over 42nd street
            radio/tv internet
NY Times   LA Times   times everywhere
Time magazine the poet laid to rest in Berkeley 1956
        time must acknowledge

*first thought best thought*
recorded shock:   the Poet is gone
        next day
            gone
        next day
            gone…
        ……………

voice out of 1950's San Francisco…

*what do you mean by naked?*

144

                    replying
took off his clothes
walked naked thru poems for more than 40 years
first in a century answered Whitman's call:

                *to those unborn...*
                *Poets to come*
                *...a new brood...*
                        *greater than*
                        *before known*
                *Arouse! For you must justify me*

he did   singing America's song

to keep those breathing alive   poetry alive
ridding language of bullshit
knocked down skeletons in their flesh...
for that pulitzer/grant committees ignored him
awarded those who never made a sound...
one official laureate's voice with different names/

                        sang past his critics
louder   he had to...

if the man sometimes failed to
live up to the poet's vision
wasn't always as wise
enjoyed his rock star status more
than we thought he should
wasn't always the person who wrote the poems
        not every poem soaring lately

isn't it enough he widened the road
wanted America to be better
all of us better...

> *I enter your secret places with my mind, I speak*
> *with your presence*
> *I roar your lion roar with mortal mouth....*

enough Whitman's child acknowledged his legacy
called out the same:

> *This ode to you O Poets and Orators to come, you father*
> *Whitman as*
> *I join your side, you Congress and American people...*

called out
next day
calling out
calling out

# What It Comes Down To

is breathing:   a poem
every week   one body
strumming another on-
to the guitar   page...
to keep breathing
kept my ballet feet
outwitting pain longer than
they did   flying
off the ground   the word
to each other
what it all comes down to
everything came down to...
knew when I had it/absolutely
and when it broke
snapped like a band in my face
and flying off the page
was flying into a void
I knew   at any cost
getting back my breath
while still breathing
what it now comes down to

# No Earthly Sense Gets It Right

by Linda Lerner

LRB 19

## Imagine the Sound of One Hand Clapping? Can You?

when my lover packed up
did what i asked
and left, it was very quiet
even when the radio and TV were on
quiet was the loudest sound
in the house
drowned out any other;
i didn't think it could
ever get any quieter than that
till the day i visited my mother
in the nursing home and
asked if she wanted
to sit in front of the TV;
she was complaining about
the head nurse, said
*I am very quiet*
i mistook for not being
any trouble; she looked
into my eyes, voice barely audible

*you don't know what it feels like*
*not to hear the sound*
*of your own voice*

i recalled how as a child
i lay in bed one night trying
to imagine what it was like
to be dead   so frightened
i wanted to cry out for help
but couldn't utter a sound/
not one sound

## Spontaneous Rant

we did it because it was easier & agreed
she'd understand if she knew what we decided
not to tell her but to do now
not then when it would be more difficult
that she'd have done it herself if there'd been time
only something felt wrong
like we were plotting a murder
the day we made arrangements
paid for it in full
so all there'd be to do is to wait
for it to be done with if it had to happen at all
wanting yes even eager
for *her own good* he said *& ours*
for it to be over with at last
but needing more time for what
i hoped to find out with time
& never my idea in the first place
being the impractical one
vindication came like a pardon   YES
when I heard from my brother that it bounced
YES   his *hell of a nerve* tone
death my mother's death bounced

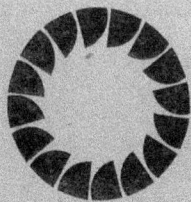

Linda
Lerner
GREATEST
HITS
1989–2002

# Construction Summer

*August 2000*

Yellow Cat trucks crack up
days on Greenwich Street
jackhammers and drills
breaking the sound barrier of thought
and everywhere people jamming in cell phones;
urban muzak I must get used to
as I watch hard hats break up
chunks of downtown history
upscaling, outpricing more than
this place I call home;

elsewhere an old woman's mind
is breaking apart in a Forest Hills nursing home
one piece at a time
echoes after me when I leave,
and doesn't stop at four pm
like the unionized noise outside...
anticipating my next apartment
the one after that and that
it is not too great a leap
to where this woman I call my mother
but who really vanished
in the outback of age, now lives...

> *"I will never..."*
> *"She said that too"* replies my brother, matter of factly...

Outside, nails pounded into wood
cobblestones hammered back into the street...

from the Bronx my lover of ten years
lost for five of them, "liquid Jesuit"/
seminary dropout, ex poet

returns with e-mail love
a decision to "Zen it" learning computer code:

no way here of being misunderstood, misinterpreted;
in this language no one get hurt...

Listen: the odor of tar poured on the street
coming in thru the windows
that churns my stomach: real
the smell of garbage compacted outside: real, too
the sanitation worker who gives me
the once over with his eyes, also real...
memory has no odor,
what flashbacks real are the rare
times we come together, eyes and hands
groping each other like mad

real is when my mother breaks thru
her mental cataracts and suddenly sees me:
    *do you have a job that pays the rent?*
    *how is it where you live?*

If she could hear me
I'd tell her
everything is in pieces
the streets, sidewalk,
dangerous to walk;
to look too hard at anything
risks a break, a misstep;
myths deconstruct without warning:
the perfect "forever" love
place called home
job that's a six month gig

156

I keep reapplying for;
everywhere I walk  buildings   trees
in metal or wooden cages,
steel cranes everywhere
and the interminable sound of drilling
following me to work and
where I used to live and live now;

to find what is rock
won't crack beneath my weight
something more than these words
than the person writing them
is to dig deeper than the men outside
but not so deep I bypass it

# Safe House: Chelsea Hotel, Room 51

I. 9/12/2001

What led me to this prewar haven
to sink into green moss
breathe in green like oxygen
be sheltered by these impenetrable green walls,
who or what should i thank
for being one of the lucky ones
after....one of the lucky ones....

..........................................................

II. 9/13/2001

To get back
is to go thru numerous checkpoints,
show ID to prove I live on Greenwich Street,
am the same woman in that photo
taken before 9/11/2001, the lie...
no straight route,
diverted this way, that
people group solitary,
white masks over parched mouths
we drift down broken cobbled streets
wheeling backpacks
                        to or away from
what there isn't any word for yet in English.
knocked into some other dimension
can only ask

              *does this subway go...*
                *how much further to*

clutching bottles of water
for our lives;
seven or eight more blocks,
air worsens; lineup of huge trucks
carrying supplies for exhausted men
in cleanup/rescue operation,
equipment to remove what
can't ever be removed;
long row of huge white satellite dishes
flower in frozen bloom on Greenwich Street;

radios explode Arabs   terrorists   Bin Laden;
red cross ladies eye witness news firemen police
in one place every place;
I adjust my mask: mouth, eyes
to see just enough
no more...

Suspicious suitcase half a block away,
and danger of gas explosions prevent us
from entering our building;
we sit on wooden boxes left outside a closed store
half a block away
and wait for the bomb squad;

see my mother seated on a similar, smaller box
in our living room after my grandmother died,

hear my father's seventeen year old hurt voice
in his aging manhood
reach past a daughter's closed ears,
boy thrown out by his own father

to join other boys
marching away from Russia's
killer army death squad....

Thru shift of wind's swirl of dust particles, debris
bits, pieces...his mother pushed into a stove,
father hid in cemeteries,
caught pneumonia   gone   gone...
...................................................
Endless trudge thru police search snow,
three years wait in Amsterdam...
America!   oh America!

Angry woman's voice criticizing someone
for tying up the free phone
with grocery shopping rug cleaning
in times like these
snaps me back to 2001

III.  9/14/2001

I force back the urge to vomit
from the odor of spoiled meat
and stench of burning of death;
take what I need from my apartment

and flee;
new immigrant's fear seizes me
when a marshal in gray uniform, high hat and boots
rifle skinned close
flinches programmed ready
when I look like I'm
trying to sneak by without showing my papers

160

have not been checked by the cop
who went for a map to assist me,
and gets back just in time;
for now I breathe easy....

..............................................................

that night, all next day I take cover
as my father did more than
half a century ago,
smoke from another world
a war we won
blows in through closed windows, decades
from my father's Russia,
sirens that struck fear in him
years after he left
blares thru my safe house
...hijacked planes fly into the same twin towers
as this city, my city burns thru
a TV screen...

...........................

I flatten my palms against the walls, press hard
into its old green, force of life green fuse
of Dylan Thomas, green spirit of
all the artists who stayed here
of Virgil Thompson, Huncke, Thomas Wolf
bury myself in green to stay alive in green....

IV. 9/15/2001

Crunch of news trucks outside my building,
Verizon, AT&T, trucks carrying huge cranes
construction material...

crowd snapping cameras at
the enormity of a lunatic's vision
that made it out,
still smoking......alive
vaporized human imprints burnt
into twisted metal and steel;

all masks off now
................................

V. 9/16-17/2001

To avoid getting lost
I go home: room 514, Chelsea,

for two days, rarely leave
except to buy food, a newspaper;
faces of the missing, everywhere,
on street poles. store windows
with me here...

VI. 9/18/2001

I walk up the wide steps of my building,
too preoccupied and too much noise
to notice construction crew at work
with drills, jackhammers
in the plaza outside;
flip the switch,
and the lights come on,
reset the VCR, clocks,
clean up the gray white hazardous dust

162

shrouds everything, and
ignorantly try using a can of Lysol
to disinfect death...

out back men continue work
on a gentrification project
begun weeks before...
first day of Rosh Ha Shona,
machines attack concrete
force green thru putrid cement mud.
to green a landlord's property,
his dirty palm....
Jew descendent of people
from my father's world,
blinded by green, inflicts pain,
on those just evacuated from their lives
to *what has to be done survival;*

a silent scream forced back all week
rose up in my throat, unleashed
all the artillery
a human heart is capable of
at these Spanish, Dominican, Pakistani immigrants
who barely understand English,
hired to do a job
to put food on their tables, feed their families
men like my father who came here with dreams
stare at me in bewilderment....

My neighbor rushes out
to calm me down....
     *nothing you can do about it*
          words

I shove aside:
*bastards, sons of bitches*
*killers,* I scream at something
elusive, too primitive
to see, hiding right in front of me,

scream to prove I'm still alive:
to be heard
above the sound of death

# Haywire

I.

They came from heartland's America
to see New York City, not a six minute
movie unwinding into a deli
where this group from Ohio
sat chomping on thick pastrami rye
mustard squirting out and
                              oh my
such a funny smell in the air...
busy gorging on New York fantasy
didn't see death rush down five flights,
feel death brush against them
with bulging knapsacks of marijuana;

felt like extras in a movie
with cops rushing about, then
something went gunshot wrong
speeded up   broke out of the film
leaving three dead bodies, two wounded
blood splattered Pollock walls
before the ladies could stop chewing
long enough to taste fear
through hot mouthfuls

II.

Four months minus a day later,
three minutes, half the time...

Happens all the time in Manhattan,
a woman gets in the way of someone's urge,
is pushed in front of a train

or struck from behind with a brick,
can never be explained
even as we do it: food, sex   need to hurt
kill what's in the way,
gives some logic comfort…
to survive we take shelter in routines
don't see what we're seeing
as we walk to trains buses
that morning may have voted first,
I did….felt the first siren's needle prick
I've grown numb to in this city of my birth,
only didn't stop this time
like some mechanism failed   broke…
a few just waking turned on the TV,
a foreign war movie in progress on our streets;
funny how fast wars can spread
a few thousand people be in the way
lines that shouldn't be crossed are:
your country/mine, borders
behind which we feel safe vanish in
in a single toast and coffee burning morning;

same movie every night now:
screams pitched too loud for
the human ear break out over the city,
same nightmare: we all know it is only a dream:
we all know we will never wake from it

# A KOAN FOR SAMSARA

## By LINDA LERNER

*These poems, written between late June 1991 and early 2003, arranged more or less chronologically, tell a love story, the kind that, if you're lucky—and I was—happens once.  Once  only.*

*"So, yeah, 'lucky,' me too, in spades, backed by guitar blues and cascading gentilities of fluttering saxophone solos in the night and pictures on the wall and in my head and 'lucky' wrapped in wordless speech, my shelter from all the cold and hurt and loneliness and no one to hear or even want to listen or stop the bleeding with some ephemeral touch, just one, you, knowing how to call back the dead not for some illusory reward, because the only thing we can ever gain is what there is in life, yeah, baby, 'lucky' doesn't even touch it…"*

*—Andrew Gettler (April 20, 2000)*

# For "A Well Travelled Ghost:" No Regrets

You can shut down   cut off
not ever think about the Nam again
what came before:   Gillespie at the Vanguard
or afterwards:   way you loved to play language
made your muted blues speak
"a joyful noise…"
you can forget all that   but
something always yanks you back:
to me:   to get you back

as in a jazz improv when
forced off-note wailing   *too soon*
certain   in   the *isn't   can't be*
there *is/was*   more;
all the beside-the-point excuses
that mattered…your legal woman   kids
addiction   obligations…really don't

when it comes to saving a soul:
what this poem is about
having no regrets   that extra breath:
and why I tried so hard to get you back

# Resurrection Poem: Easter, 2000

An atheist discredited:
how else to explain
my lover's emerging from
vodka drowning death
dry and touch-of-flesh alive
with my hands   mouth
trying to disprove
and unable...
death we both agreed on
signed invisible certificates;
an illegal widow   I went out
in my gypsy clothes
wandering thru cities   a nomad
flinging out magic tokens   mantras
disguised as poems to
lure you back
burying you with those same words
before strangers who applauded:
once I conjured you back
in another man   believed in my own magic
till his lips   hands
wrote nothing on my body
in such precise braille   **nothing**
his curious stranger's eyes trying
to figure out what...nothing
it was nothing;
thought my mind was getting even
when intimations of your life
began teasing me on a computer screen
just as my five years of mourning ended;
but when you broke down virtual barriers
lifted me in your arms
through beaded curtains
carried me to bed
as if no time at all passed
I knew   in real time
it hadn't

# In Soldier Slang

*for Andrew*

> "...and i took
> the kiss
> you wanted..." —Andrew Gettler

the flash-to-bang time
must be quick,
old soldier of many wars
you knew better than anyone...
first intimation:
coughed out in Pall Mall smoke,
not here   not yet...

Thirty years back   Vietnam:
*my eyes burned holes*
*thru the jungle,*
*looking for death, hoping*
*to see it before*
*it saw me...* *

followed you to California;
you kicked it off
in shivering cold dark
and returned home:
urban street violence
didn't frighten you
or much of anything now,
let down your guard
and it sprang out of
uncorked Bronx nights
almost drowning you in 100 proof years;
dried off over two decades.
You got into the habit of
thinking alive,

171

comfortable with the concept
of your own mortality
BANG   through
your right arm  chest
BANG   ambush lasted
three chilled days before
you grabbed hold of me
and broke free.
............................................

How many lovemaking times
did you die in my arms trusting
you'd come back   and again...
............................................

The last two years
we homed naked in cyber space
your mind fleshed  through
my everyday    got me through
each tedious battle

the futility of anyone   my mother
outliving her mind
gave you a way
to speak of it
sparing me  us.
............................................................
In all the selfless
selfishness of great love,
I gave you the time I wanted.

# A Koan for Samsara

*"Cling to truth and it becomes falsehood;*
*understand falsehood and it becomes truth.*
*…two sides of a coin"*
                    *—Ryokan*

Who else but a guy with a Jesuit mind
who believed koan answers are the only ones
would leave me two dates for his death—
others ghost through and
one you rose from
inhabiting the name, Samsara
in a cyber home,

tell me,
when you died and I didn't know for four months
and four months later when I did,
                    which one
the bureaucrat's single blow
with an official stamp
                    or
one ripped through my body
made my soul bleed as only you
knew a soul could

and your vodka drowning death taught me:
the boundary blurred between
what was flesh and wasn't;
pain from an amputated part
I couldn't locate   name
like now   relentless….
went through the motions of a job   a life,
everyone who saw me never did,

173

pain hollowed five years....
One who called himself Samsara came to me;
I sniffed out your mind's scent
in his denials...the rhythm
of your being, way your breathed thought
through my bodyhead
to tell me
            tell me

which one?

# Eleven Years

*for Andrew, once again*

So unlikely a bluebird would
cross my window to pause
on such a dreary November day
I didn't see it go...

Thanksgiving eve
your death flew
across my computer screen.

# From the Fire

the fire girls jumped off
a factory roof to escape
trapped over 100 others   20 years before
my mother, a millinery copyist in
another factory could smell the smoke
whenever anyone spoke of
someone they knew...

*worse than what there couldn't ever be*
*anything worse...*she said;

                           words
I walked past   though
ignorant of the embers

                   long before
you fleshed out of my fantasy
and after   even after

I smelled it   awful
like nothing I had ever known
couldn't get away from,
you knew instinctively, whose lungs
40 years of Pall Mall smoke blackened;

                  death's crackling
I couldn't hear in my mother's words
or stop hearing now
blocks from where I lived...

...kept seeing that sky, crowded with so many
from so high to fall
my mother couldn't have imagined

176

as flame winged
they flew down
90 years ago

how many more would fly
even further down
one at a time
slam into the earth,

*couldn't ever be anything worse...*

But I know now
what you did...
there's no bottom to anything
                    always

        "still a down and
    further still to fall and faster than i
        thought..."

twin-souled   and yet
10 months before
I had—there was...urned proof,
as you talked me safely out
of lower Manhattan through our life
back to Brooklyn
loved me past mortal flesh

I didn't even have a clue...

you were already speaking to me
        from the fire.

# An Off the Wall Protest
*February 2003*


Decades ago, returning vet
you flung your medals at the White House,
I fling words on a page now   another war
you'd be protesting with me
if I wasn't protesting your death.

Learned in Vietnam
to know the real enemy   the dead:
marching into jungle swamp deserts
reciting *the lord is my shepherd*
the dead: we surrender our souls to every day.

You saw with your own mind
heart's eye   didn't need
a politician doctor bossman
telling you how to live
breathe compromise   or **when**
death had you in its chokehold...

having known Long Bînh Jail's torture[1]
you wouldn't accept a medicine man's for
some zero quality time.

Your penis computer animated
my coffee mornings
those last months...
    *see how big alive—*
and growing even bigger and
*"wanting is the hottest sweetest thing you know"* [2]
outlasting every kind of war
all the broken promised moments we had
and couldn't keep....

so when your daughter wrote ,
*he passed away*
wasn't you, my love…a dead goodsoldierman I saw

or ever see…
not you at all

# In This Non-Afterwards

I can touch you tuning every nerve
touching me   start
soft drum rolls pulsing
coax treble notes from
    my breasts thighs
hear you playing your bluesbaby again

                can you hear
those high clitoral notes
screaming out your name   andrew
lick after lick tonguing through death's door

hear it andrew   do you hear
your cock filling me
the hottest poem in town promise
        I gave you before
I knew   it would come afterwards

1992

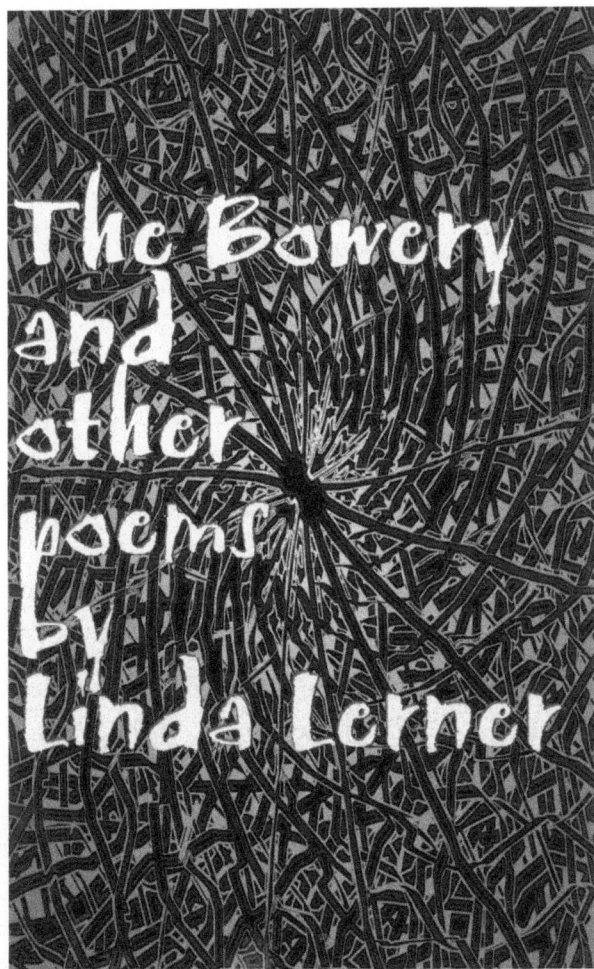

from *The Bowery and Other Poems*

# Brooklyn Unmapped

Saturday morning drills into sleep
begins to cover up cracks   widen sidewalks/
outside my window:  gentrification
in full force on Greenwich Street;
and the past
synonymous with lie
finds a way to bypass:
Brooklyn shadows Manhattan skyline;
what the hell am i doing here?
ten minutes by subway
a truckload of boxes unpacked
as fast as it takes
as fast as
Dylan Thomas' owls
snuck in bearing it away
long before i opened my eyes
in this Manhattan of a girl's Brooklyn dreams
that was Eden my Fern Hill
a prince fast horse riding
to snatch me off...

not where four of us
climbed tenement walls to escape
from each other/ourselves
the poverty of something unspoken
but an unmapped Brooklyn where i rode
high on word visions/on love
all day every night rode
with my lover

to wake up years later
alone on Greenwich Street
taste of him still on my tongue
words dead on page to prove/
seven days cracking concrete
planting trees   to make a Paris boulevard
where a Jewish child-woman
waits for someone to
christen this place: home
start a history going

## TriBeCa Walking Song:
## Crossing Over Gets Me Back Anyway I Work It


heading down Greenwich Street
old factory-look warehoused
for lofts going fast at a million plus
cross cobblestone fragments
of romanticized age, if
i don't smell the horse shit
time cleansed...but i do
turn left and
reach the Hudson River—
isn't the East River i lived near
walked along with my lover...
if i really walk far enough
bits of our past
play hide and seek in the
shadows of iron gratings;
i choose not
to smell his vodka breath
on the raw wind and keep walking

pass trucks marked
gourmet garbage disposal;
*there goes the neighborhood*—
a gourmet bodega   pizza—
words used in my Flatbush Brooklyn childhood
where nobody had but
tumbled out when someone *other*
moved in, called mockey whose
English broke on their tongues;
my mother a Russian immigrant's wife
born here   registered democrat

with others like her named
who didn't vote   weren't
100% real Americans: the odd
that throw off a neighborhood
like these triangle streets
i delight in...

to get home
i must keep walking

# A New Sound of Being

No musician, I can
only string words to poem
my soul's ache
        but
I've played some bad notes
took an improv wrong turn
yanked off the shroud facts become
           afterwards
to keep one from vanishing who said

    *no one ever does anything*
    *for someone else's good*

    right/wrong...

on the steps of the Brooklyn courthouse
    a crowd gathers
a jazz band out of Brighton Beach
is tuning up the July heat...

I sit among them tossing around
an invisible coin
    wrong/right

a Nigerian bass player, Latino guitarist
sax player from....I forget
slides off Russian tongued English intros
and a man riding the **A train**
out of St. Petersburg two weeks
jumpin' miles of decades
    at a keyboard
      thru America
more than my Russian father traveled

187

in 50 years  on that dream journey
he died before completing
I'm making in ways
he never imagined
might not have approved

...the Russian is playing
freedom's sound across new prairie land
where concrete truths mean nothing
and it was  ALL  right,
everyone  breathing a new sound of being
when a fire engine crashes through
notes flung everywhere
derailing us in its
clanging rush
to save lives;

the band played thru the sirens
relentless...
took some minutes and then
sax man  his timing perfect  stepped forward
        blowing soft & sweet
smile spread across
the keyboard cat's face  he
picks up the sound  and then the
Nigerian  pulling tough strings
        slow & easy
            yeah
        all of them now
        and this time
        it was
    EVERYTHING  was
        all right

            yeah

# State of Mind: Cloud in a Makebelieve Sky

I turn on/up
jazz as a dam   a levee
to hold back the onslaught of ugliness;
tried it with Miles
after the toilet   bathtub overflowed
sewage spoiling through my apartment,
but he's way too cool/polite
so maybe Prez or Ornate
but they cannot get out the odor;
even after someone comes in to sanitize
and a neighbor says   *it's gone now/*
isn't   another sense picks it up,
something more wrong than the plumbing
construction work outside...
This is no place to dream;
my neighbor says   *home is a state of mind,*
she blocks out the noise...
I cannot put my books   photos
in a state of mind
and tell me, how do you separate
Miles from his trumpet
the poet from the space she breathes in
her soul wailing through it
one flowing into the other
how do you avoid contamination
in this apartment   this city
        this life
tell me   how do you separate
    how do you
        how

# One of the Ten Best

One blue sky week in September
the sun didn't burn or leave me
wanting to take the chill out
and the dying which began 2001
had come to a halt: been months
and no one...
seven days my lover would have called
one of the 10 best for each
if he were still here;
I kept seeking out the sun
any vacant bench on the promenade
overlooking the East River,
a few hours storing up ammunition
because soon
                    the second anniversary would strike
and all day in New York City across America
the dead would be killed one by one.

# The Bowery

What drove a man all the way from Puerto Rico
to New York slum promise: a home
enough bread and meat to still
the gnawing inside only
didn't feed the soul's belly
vicarious lusts of a public
who wanted blood,
what it cost him,

film about this Puerto Rican poet
who bled on paper:
*I do bad things so I can write about them*
with me as I left the cinema, walked down
blocks in metal lockup, graffiti ravings
bouncing off foreclosed immigrant dreams,

men like my father who
opened one store after another
to salvage minimum wage lives
behind a cash register,
lose what they
never imagined having....

No place for a woman alone
where streets mattressed homeless bodies
forever in imagination
and a knife in my back might be only
as far away as someone's hunger,
who'd kill for a greasy meal
easily as a farmer slaughters
a pig a chicken to survive;

but gentrification danger is new safety
where tenement rents
skyscrape believe in trendy poverty;

walked past where the sidewalk abruptly curved
thru a gate...once vacant lot
over farmland owned by
New Amsterdam's governor,

meanders a grove of birch trees
herbs, berries...piece of.
the original Bouwerie

grabbed out of stinking garbage centuries later
by green guerrilla fighters for $1.00 a month....
wildflower dreams of those who
risked their forgotten lives
to leave something
...hundreds of perennials of varieties
flowering right here now,
sprung out of this very soil

## On Meeting Ray Bremser in Cherry Valley, 8/7–8/9/98

they say he was an outlaw
robbed some banks   did time
a poet who dug out
with words made tools
instruments he used to
play his own kind of jazz
*they say   they say*
three months before he died
barely fleshed skeleton
i met in Cherry Valley
voice cutting thru late summer green
w/gravely sand   rocks
hurt to listen…
i didn't see   nobody did
a man clinging to a cliff
behind his dark glasses & cowboy hat
cut up   bloody   spitting out
nonstop SOS   all weekend
we unwittingly answer

# What Is It About

the word *still*, when someone asks
am i *still*, wants to know
same anything...apartment/job
makes me want to slam it against a wall:
still doing the usual, eating at the same diner,
watching the news: 10:00 pm/11:00,
*are you still*, alone/together
complaining about it   *still*...
decide to skip out:
another address, further than moving
from Brooklyn to Manhattan
flying west, than some can imagine:
*why?   what happened?*
as though i had announced a death
any death...
don't they know
i'm not *still* living here
not the person who moved in,
am *still* the woman who can't
let her man go, who isn't *still*
the one she fell in love with
and is, always will be,
make them see
the utter ridiculousness of
this hunt for a myth/*still*

# Down These Metaphysical Streets I Walk Naked & Unseen

i am an outsider   recognizable by
my camera eye stare
knapsack and long gypsy skirt
walking down Essex   Rivington   Lower
East Side New York

here is anywhere i'm walking down
those silent metaphysical streets
i've walked down too many times
lost and alone in
New York   New Mexico   New Orleans   Colorado
forgotten towns across America
dim lit, shadowy, as in some
noir cinema of another time
walked down the exact moment
i've walked, as now
down these hot July streets

a smell i inhaled in Williamsburg, the Bronx
a noveau poverty baked
into the bricks and sidewalk
vibrating with truck rumble car horn
blast children's screams flying
thru salsa sounds melting hot
ice cream yearnings in the air;

want to tear off my clothes
forget i'm already naked if
someone bothers to look....

i pass a group of tattooed Latinos

giggling teenage girls
hormonally bursting out of white shorts
a man reading the want ads on a stoop
dreaming new world in the old Spanish tongue

walk another block and come
to an impasse: a truck and crowds
blocking off the street, low budget
filmmakers here to steal something to
bargain for that original dream

too many depressions wiped away
for it ever to vanish entirely
                            from imagination;

like love.  What have i to bargain with?
except need?  offer it to a passerby
who has that hungry look
i recognize

          *hey you,*
*cost only a few hours    a few words*

once on a Greenwich Village corner
in a hotel lobby
in cyber space, on a page
sunlightlaughter tore up those streets
and once undressed past
where i thought possible
and once   took years
could strike once again/make
poverty a word

tenemented in lower east side New York
where a job pays rent, buys enough
tacos and enchiladas to fill
a hungry belly   banish it
from their lives

a town i'm passing through

Because You Can't I Will

Linda Lerner

# Instructions:

*"come...*
*finish...."*
—Andrew Gettler, *"Liquid Jesuit"*

Never
    to have known DNA exists in words as
    in nails & hair & blood

    broken its code and felt death's pulse
    in your arms   to have been so lucky...
            *come...*
            *finish...*
as though you knew what you couldn't
possibly have known a decade before
but did

using all your Jesuit mind-strength
kept taking on death to prove you could outwit it
as your hard drinking Irish grandfather did
into his '90s...

Never
    doubted you   who'd survived Nam
    Bronx street wars, vodka drowning   couldn't...

to have been so lucky
Never
    to have known when you torched that angry blast:

        *Don't want you*
        *coming to my poem*
        *finishing my poem*

with those gentle words   *come*  *finish*
you were giving me a reason to breathe on:

instructions for afterwards.

## The Poem   The Rare Soul

the ones who fire off a page
I can hear   almost touch   smell

like my lover's scent gets inside
whose spirit was fleshed: bled   hurt

kept riding its rhythm toward the poem
he heard wordless every waking moment

the rare ones who make me see
in everything that's flawed   isn't there

everything they can be   and now are
because they've shown me

the only ones worth having—
like breath   must be let go

# The Ferry & Other Matters

I must haul something up
from the wreckage
and poem it
      fast
         before
it's lost in
the gull winged death cries
New York's winds unleash
bodies   severed limbs
bobbing up & down  investigations

what my father must have seen
when he looked out across the river
thru the cold glass steel
before he got off the boat:
I am an immigrant's daughter
and I saw it too

the last summer we could afford
to pay only a nickel or dime to ride the ferry
...the poet Connellan's yacht
days he pulled a hand truck thru
thief snatching streets before
I met him   he introduced us
and the towers immortalized our world.

I was waiting for you
to find me;
the black gold night
had the sweetest sound,
the air just right and
we were both still alive.

from the top deck you watched the gulls
swoop into limitless waters thirsting
your imagination with vodka
out of sight I saw blind-sighted;
hands held, we sat among foreign visitors
those who'd left work for a party lunch
or had no work or
just needed to take this ferry.....
                ......
*The captain must have been drunk or blacked out*
*they say....things like this don't just happen...*
*why is it taking so long?*

*Dead numbers pile up body bagged*
*in newsprint   digitalized   on TV*
*more ammo   more big guns firing every day.*
                ......
To dredge up empty bottles   years of cigarette butts
a weeping wife   angry children
flowerpot flung across a room one drunken night
explains nothing....

we're long gone from that boat
bearing your name
nobody pays even a nickel to ride anymore
and we couldn't afford after that summer
ghosted off streets
we touristed in our city
sat in an old graveyard
reading names fading into stone:
                                those
who were and aren't
when we were us
and saw everything with new eyes

# What's Missing   Is
*for Donald Lev*

*(who misses his typer)*

what the typer[1]
gave us:   percussion
to hear the heart's steady beat
outside in   side out   side in...

I knew a woman once, a writer
whose child fell asleep to it
and on off nights when
she wasn't working would bawl
till she'd start
hitting those keys;

wordman knew he could fly
off the flat earth
not fall through time

                same
as any jazz cat   when
there's someone to
keep time for him...

I don't have a typer anymore.
What I have is
the memory of a man's voice...
backgrounds everything I do;

if I take the words out,
ones already spoken and the ones
that can't ever be
I hear it so truly   a heart
beating through death
            right through

205

# I Call Him Sam

my year old gray/white cat stares at a sparrow
from the windowsill
his big green eye   the other tearing   shrunken
infected months before he came here

hungers after what he can't have
but will get   the way
we do when something is prohibited...

mornings:   that familiar cry for foodlove
blanket against the cold even in hottest summer
wakes me   and

I bury my own needs
to give him what
can no longer be given to me

feel each rib of his tiny body
I move my hand across
rubbing my forehead in his fur
that warms us both...

*Sam*  I say   not Samsara
the name you took before you knew
the wheel was turning its last round

...our first sleeplessnight morning
I woke to find you on the coach
and thinking something wrong
lay down beside you
your penis rose up   *like a fish*   I said
licking it   both of us smiling
                                    in flight

and I remember how afterward it fell across my thigh
I stroked it and that purring look you had
unmapping injuries from lives
before ours began....

*his name is Sam* I say just Sam

## Once Only for Sailors & Hot Shots on Motorcycles

Have you seen the man with a tattooed face
      holding a needle
through a 6th avenue store window
        been curious
     gone in   watched
the women searching thru
pictures same as the men
finally choose one
         almost
feels like the wild thing beating inside,

wondered about this man
no priest  that's for sure   but
maybe way he holds the needle
someone looking up at him
         so trusting
gives it a baptismal feel...

*you pay for what you get*   he says
to the the old questions:
...cannot guarantee what he doesn't hear;

I have seen bodies flowered   initialed
bragging peace signs   crosses   stars   oms
wings fluttering on legs
waists coiled by snakes grown
bigger more elaborate

like the flag   everywhere now
no body sees anymore...

I have
a kundalini   fire snake coiled
at the base of my spine someone's fingers
inched nail by nail one night;
A kiss-burn winged on my stomach
suns from a lover's touch

those gone imprinted forever
on nerve & bone....

why would I want my body to speak
someone else's vision?

# Street Jazz/Blues thru Summer Hot

when it's not there   if I can't find
someone wailing out of a sax
hear a low down trumpet moan
guy singing the blues on a street corner
my mind curls up into itself
the heat is gone from summer
there's no perspiration to wipe away
the kind that comes after two people
have been diving into each other all night
and ride out sticky wet to the bone....
I drag thru the tedium of
thick heavy days in which nothing flies
....it was in summer
I first learned to fly
the air blew out of a thousand saxophones
one June   a soul breath note
I could almost touch   feel its hot flesh
burning inside   and
June went on for years

## Zen Cat

I like that it's simple with him
what he wants doesn't road off
in circle blind alleys   I can't see past
anger claws out in a whip lash
                          and gone
love  unconditioned to games we play
have their own space-time
I like that it doesn't get complex
as it did with us sometimes
how he looks at me when I speak
goes deep inside words he can't comprehend
& pulls out meaning
at their exact nerve-pitch   how
what was always becomes what is
dragged into our now
I like that he reminds me of
us when we were
undressed way past clothes
& how we got back there at the end…
I like that he reminds me

*These poems are for Nina Howes,*
*who's been here & knows the route*

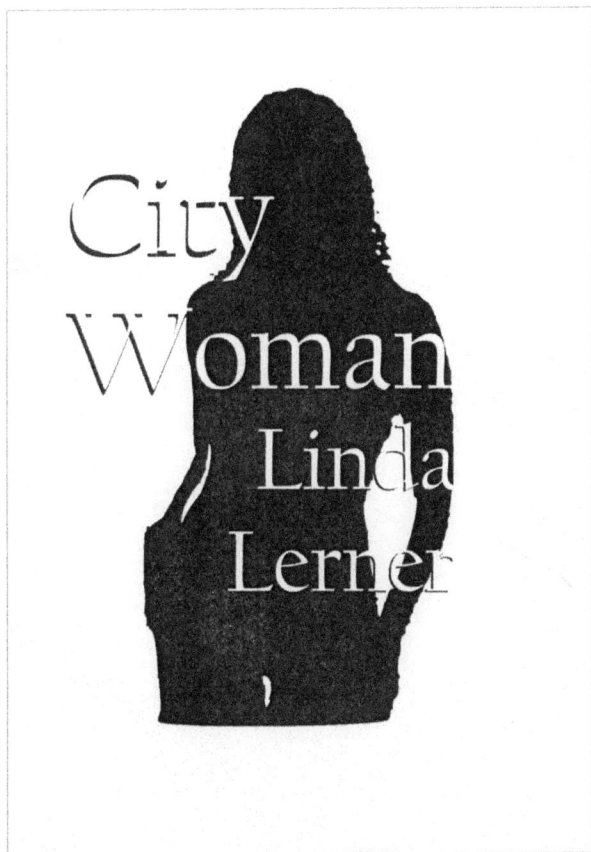

City
Woman
Linda
Lerner

# Roadmap: For New York City
# Turn Left at the First Mirage

hit me as I watched workman gut out
the insides of a four floor brownstone
from my bedroom window
leaving the frame

what happened to this city
I was twice born in
whose familiar signature
scrapped the skies of my youth
blown up   left this terrible gap
I stare thru to possibilities
that once towered like babel...

the Arabs didn't strike the first blow
they only woke us up...

I was waiting for something
this city promised me
no different from those I mocked
hooked up like patients on life support
who couldn't see what they didn't hear

& railed against Union Square's
bargain hunting humanity
massed in one grotesque "I love New York" t-shirt
out noising boom boxes that once fired
thru the streets

...I remember blowing up at a guy for
taking me into Nathan's 42nd street
before going to the theater

...had the best franks I ever ate
I admitted later when
SoHo & Little Italy began to have the same glossy look
& it was getting harder
to tell the difference between virtual & real;
stupid   bad   disabled   vanished from our vocabulary
               not the city...
no body could afford to live
in the old neighborhood words anymore;

Auden once said "we must love one another or die;"
people chose not to die
pretended to love one another & stopped living...

my bank became a customer relationship center
abstinence was the latest god
I rebelled against in new love's sanction
before it went up in 40 years of Pall Mall smoke
taking my city with it...

I've walked thru
Times Square's new family approved streets
emptied of peep shows
out of towners once slouched into
passed health food places   expensive restaurants
...there's still McDonalds
but no Nedick's   no Howard Johnson's where everyone
went for great ice scream sundaes   huge pies
& pigged out on enormous meals or
those small diners on Broadway/tucked between 7th & 8th
whose 80 cent cups of coffee never left
Starbucks' bitter aftertaste for twice the amount—

———————————————

Dec. 27, 2005  heading down 42nd & 7th
toward the A train home
I passed a lineup of food stands
outside stores selling pricey sport clothes
people ate and drank from large coffee cups
jammed in so tight it was like
a river rose up over the new urban levees...

next day I watched the ice skaters in Rockefeller Center
& let the tree overwhelm my cynicism;
in other's eyes saw what I couldn't
    & for a moment

what once skylined unbroken
across a girl's vision/a woman
lingering on the corner of St. Marks & 8th
    a man she'd just met
& what might never happen again
    YES   IT WAS   YES
    for a moment now
in one blinking light's breath..../
    won't

# The Gateway

*The Gates, Central Park, NYC, Feb. 12-28, 2005*

when things got so bad
we couldn't take it anymore
a sinkhole formed beneath this city
and we fell thru

gray air flamed….my eyes tasted
what wafered on my tongue
warmed me inside and
smiled out on hundreds of
thousands rescued
                this winter
a fire had knocked out a couple of subway lines
plunging us deeper into the cold
I trudged thru for days
to find an exit  some way out

a gunman holding up a group
on familiar Bowery blocks
grabbed a woman's dare: "What are you gonna do, shoot us?"
along with her purse…

a sinkhole 23 miles big…

…called saffron
but it was orange & who cared what
ignited everything to get us out of where we were

flowed thru me down this park's footpaths
as a woman I'd been warned to stay off
and fell thru gate after gate
into an otherworldliness…

someone gone   ghosted by in the shadows
of fabric & imagination...

I climbed some rocks   & looked down:
what was stolen from us
two foreign artists returned
salvaged from our fears

did what all the cops had failed to accomplish;
it was as temporary as life itself...

I felt sorry for those
who couldn't find the entrance
saw thousands of gates   no gateway

criticized Christo & Jeanne-Claude
who said   "it doesn't mean anything"
because it didn't

# Chicago

It's dust in my mouth
taste of the prairie's hot wind
tells me I'm in Chicago
not New York
                    days after flying in
over Lake Michigan....
A familiar looking skyline
mile of shop names i recognize
mean nothing
when the wind starts up...

long road of blocks
I'm told to walk one way
then the other to get where i want
swallows my definition of street

turning the corner
I'm in San Francisco stretched out
North Beach last June
but no...this is Chicago, flat
as the earth   *"A"*   sound and
wide open skyline,
I remind myself;

                    ...every morning
e-mail a man I love from my past,
sometimes see him here
as I almost see masked men on horseback
coughed up by the fog-wind
riding down the railroad tracks
from the old El's wooden station

and blues
coming out of every doorway   park
rough edged hard
*hurts so bad I want to cry*
*but get tough instead* blues...
Chicago, where bestbeef steak in town
is always served   Capone still
rests on the piano of his Green Mill hangout
...I read my own *don't give a damn go it alone*
*right back* blues...

takes a long time to arrive someplace new

## All The Magick There Is

That 40 something woman
scribbling in a cheap rent studio
around dead end job-
years vanishing into black holes
whose book finally makes it into the world
the woman decades ago whose
first let-blood stained promises:
she held out
dammed up her lust with a wish
released it with another/unheard
prays this book born of flesh & soul
be penetrated   a wild gypsy earth-
mother rescued from oblivion
not as one
long ago night beneath a sandy boardwalk
her body pierced
she lay like a fish harpooned
& the boy   clueless   to the woman
stretched out so contentedly it seemed...
must not be allowed to die soundless on a shelf
by those who judge   too deaf
to hear with their eyes
have not held it up to their nerves
like a shell   heard past its mundane subject:
a desperate pulse beating
a woman's oceanic cry

# TriBeCa Blues
## A Migrant Blues

Might have come out of
the Mississippi Delta but
for an accident of geography
Whitman's spirit blowing strong
off the river   along pier 25

a blues rising out of nowhere
that ghosts thru me…

I come here at twilight
to sit in this converted ship deck above the Hudson
the river on one side
volleyball sand courts, the other,
go down and walk around splintery picnic tables
get something to eat at a wooden food shack
students run   sell cheap
come here to forget:
what has been   is being destroyed,
*a hippie place*   friend Nina called
something she couldn't name
and just did;
across the west side highway   a few blocks off
is where I now live
immigrated from east river Brooklyn, a greenhorn
my Russian born father might have called me;
didn't know what home was
till I left…
construction
drilled   hammered   banged

to improve the neighborhood *they* said,
*they* who always come to civilize
*for our own good*–excuse  outprice and rob us;
an American blues rising above jackhammer assaults...

I took to the streets  cafes
a nomad shouting, wailing moaning
from the tips of my nerves my fingers
page after page  the blues  12 bars
beating back to brownstone Brooklyn
love that birthed me second and most real
love birthplace of my first joyful blues
page after page
               before I ever heard of this place
     .................
called TriBeCa: had no name
30 years ago, hardly any stores
freedom's cry rode the '60s wind
                 off the Hudson
through empty lots
deserted factory streets
just below Canal where
weeds sprung thru cracks;
egg and cheese white aproned men
loaded trucks in  *kind of blue*  mornings
and traffic's faint buzz sounded
off the West side highway...
deserted dark, ghost winds
and too many sudden night alleys

scared off criminals
attracting outlaw spirits
hauling canvasses  paints  typewriters  guitars

up steep walk up lofts
unheated and cold from high river winds
blowing in thru loose windows;
landlords grateful for any rent
ignored these strange gypsies
putting down stakes in this urban outpost...

round about anytime at all
an unspoken blues
to make a living   raise a kid
trek to a grocery store   laundromat
start a park   a green market   on sidewalk
once farmed communities,
be an artist   a person
a joyous blues
pouring onto canvasses
strumming into the streets
around piles of discarded brick
loose garbage

this pioneering city blues
sprung from the Delta
the same from the concrete   metal and steel
as from the earth   the trees
the same finding its way into cyber space now
whatever's untouched   untarnished
in us or outside
an anonymous migrant blues...

So I come to the river/pier 25
around twilight
to hear   not forget

my own blues
born near another river
from love, uncultivated
as this land   this place
called TriBeCa
I now live in
once was

the blues that brings me back
gives me hope
to make a life
to love   lose and love again
blues that doesn't end with loss
a Robert Johnson    Gatsby blues
that reaches out and out

the blues
that can't be gentrified
bought off
sold at all:

the blues
that's still alive
in me

## Tell Me What You Want
## and It Can't Be Given

I wish he had a paper cup
& threw out the old line
like the others do
beg for what can be measured
cost the price of a meal
is the size of a room
not just stand there silently
in front of White Castle
forcing me to pass him
to & from the subway
even catch myself looking around
if I don't see him
always in that same dirty tan jacket
his big eyes pooling with impenetrable darkness...
last Sunday he held a cup in his hand
another rested on a slab of concrete
he leaned against/both closed...

Damn you! your silence is asking for too much...
If I could make someone
rise up from his ashes
unmyth the phoenix
If I could do it & believe it is happening
I could give you the things that
hurt too much for words....

# Retro 20th Century Ghost

could pass for one of us
in her faded jeans & Indian clothes
if we don't look too closely...

needle marks track her body back
to 1968: long blond haired

chick with flowers in her eyes
up to psychedelic visions in mud
                    who danced
as high as the pills would swallow her
                    that whole weekend

should have woken up in
the same clothes she went to sleep in
                    shouldn't she
not those she never saw before

the question keeps asking her
she throws back at us

what happened in that black hole of oblivion
the night she went to sleep in one outfit   one century
one body to wake up in another...

funny how i.v.'s leave the same kind of marks
as those other needles
nothing changes with everything changing

pills she once took to fly off the earth
she now takes to stay on it

# Nothing Is Just

an old sound from
outside our downtown Manhattan apartment
four years later breaks thru
a Brooklyn garden a few feet
from my window
freshly dug earth   a hole
easy to slip/fall into
a grave that doesn't exist....

two years after jack hammers
began breaking up concrete foundations
every percussive bang
signaled his worsening cough
as in a macabre end of century
call & response

he reminded me of
his chain smoking hard drinking Irish grandfather
who lived into his '90s

realty developers spoke of improving
the neighborhood   ripped up trees
to plant benches

hip hop night voices broke thru sleep
angry words coughed out of our windows
worsened....

we visited the poets' cemetery in Wakefield
impressed by that huge rock marking Emerson's grave
said he might prefer burial to cremation
in case he wanted to come back...

that was before
ashes   enough to fill thousands of urns
descended on our streets
and they couldn't put out the fires for months…

I'm back in brownstone Brooklyn now
face a garden

as in our first apartment
no building higher than five floors here
careful not to get too close to anyone

                    got a cat…
that was two years later
& I was beginning to forget…

my landlord says
it will be a beautiful house
when I complain of the noise

every bang brings back what's gone without
returning it   rips thru tense

like that rope workers put up
to divide their property from this one
a strong wind keeps pulling down

dirt flies against my windows
so I can't see clearly anymore…

most people I know have stopped smoking
& some who never did
are still dying of lung cancer...

I'm not sure where
        I'm going
                in this poem
                        this life

scared when my cat coughs/throws up
the vet says it's just hairballs
but nothing is just....

**ANDREW**
    "Somewhere in Brooklyn
           in Paradise"

    —Hayden Carruth, "The Hyacinth Garden"
                *(written after visiting us)*

2007

from *Living in Dangerous Times*

# LIVING IN DANGEROUS TIMES

LINDA LERNER

# And the Bones Pile Up

> *"You would think the fury of aerial bombardment*
> *Would rouse god to relent...the infinite spaces*
> *Are still silent."*
> —Richard Eberhart
> *"The Fury of Aerial Bombardment"*

heard Allen's howl thru Whitman's leaves, 150 years thick
    mark an anniversary
as another poet's World War II bombs
 explode on the 7th day of the 7th month in London
"calling up the darkness once again,"
worst since...noted...not the holy number
laid to rest...

twenty-five years after a door gunner
poet saw Asian skies set aflame
he brought me to the Black Wall
so I could feel what a number is
when it's broken down to names;

he placed my finger over his
tracing one name...Knutson...engraved
on a red bracelet he wore,
    man he never met,
told me to press down hard,
I felt its bones thru his
hard & cold   *press harder* he said
*harder...*

poet whose memories "arc & fuse"
across decades blackened my downtown Manhattan skies
& other names I didn't have to touch
to feel the bones
smell the stink breathed
in & out of lungs for a century
rise up infiltrating a new one

235

# The Good German

*I do what I'm told,* he said,
suspecting I don't

so I lied...

For a paycheck, to survive
breathe in my own rhythm,
the reason he came here,
stepson of high-up Nazi
he ran from decades ago...
got away,
never questioned how far;
has he forgotten,
have they all                                    .
whose words, *I do what I'm told,*
echo off walls across America,

the price paid:
boys who died without
leaving a trace of themselves behind
so we could think outside the lines
between the lines,
don't always have to march on the same line;

as if someone powdering our air
with Anthrax...just a bit...
to give us a whiff of death
amid worries of a possible smallpox outbreak
isn't enough to fear

...and the whole world heading toward
another slaughtering binge.

# An American Sound

my West Indian neighbor rides an imaginary horse
across his landed fantasy
squeezed between two buildings
on a vacant lot

turning in the huge cement rollers
as the clock turns toward his settlement money

lists of foreclosed buildings
tease him from a computer screen
cushions his physical pain
day something slipped in his back
while making a delivery
and all the days with nothing to do but think
slipped out of being grateful just to have a job
why he's here not back in the Islands
he loves more than he'll ever love this country—

my neighbor's window   adjacent to mine
faces another building being gutted & rebuilt
a floor higher to rent out
wakes me not him every morning at 7 am

the sound he hears is louder than
a drill or jackhammer

is what
my father heard in Amsterdam
waiting three years for entrance to this country
half a century ago
kept hearing in failed business after business
the sound of the dollar bill
thunder of a hundred thousand dollars
purchasing his freedom…

from a green truck
the owner's voice whips down
on his workers who aren't new immigrants
like my 20 something neighbor
claiming squatter's rights
on his 40 acres of fantasy earth

too many hungry years
cut scars across their minds
too deep to let their own voices
blast thru our windows
turn up the volume on their radio

people complain   slam down windows
nobody hears anybody—

when my father came home after
cashing other people's needs in
a grocery store all day
he'd out scream the words he didn't own
to say what I couldn't hear
through all that noise

you know how it is when something
gets struck in your throat—

feels like trying to cough up what
I have no memory of swallowing

# Born at Sea Level

whole time I was in New Mexico
  I had trouble breathing
and water   I couldn't get enough of
dried off before I even got out of the shower,

ten years since I've been back;
this isn't my soul's home…

they say if you listen you'll hear
the ancient spirits speaking to you,
I didn't hear anything except

the voices of those trying to sell it
burning from incense woven into rugs & baskets
baked into pottery…dream catching longings
for something nameless

could have been when it got so cold
so suddenly in Santa Fe one April day
& hail balls startled a few who looked around
                              as if almost/but no

more likely just a natural climatic change…

wasn't in Albuquerque or Santa Fe back then
                              but in Taos
I climbed up to see where the Anasazi once lived;
  could do it so easily before
I knew how people can just disappear
  what it means for a whole tribe to vanish,
when I still had enough breath to fight nature with;

a friend drove me to the Sandia Crest
   where lifts take you even higher
but I was already so high up I touched bottom
   as never at sea level

as if we need our bodies to remind us
   where we're from
how that place we're born in gets inside
way those who architect our world
become that place;

I felt lucky I could still return
to one of them....

# I Am Asked to Believe

I am asked to believe in monster fish
predators of the sea who
will eat anything can live on land
for three days
small killers, frankenfish
who could change our ecosystem
I've seen in the hands of Chinese merchants
and find it difficult
until I recall the animal-life I met
in universities with PhDs who cut
open a person so bloodlessly polite
he soon forgets he was the prey
of those who now dress his wounds.

# The Fall

When her hearing died and
she lost the words for things,
daughter became sister;
she spoke to her first-born
in spite of the word, better,
and to the son she called brother,
sometimes husband,
heard more with her eyes
than with that damn hearing aid
she kept losing till
we stopped bothering her with it...
After the FALL four years ago
when she couldn't get up
from her living room floor...
two days before a neighbor
smelled an odor...
our mourning began
imperceptible as her falling,
her struggle to eat food
she stopped tasting
to please us,
falling...so light...so feather
broke her hip and rambled
lost in 93 year old countryside;
her eyes flagged us down.
When we left she waved;
a smile teared her face.

After they brought her back
from the hospital and back again,
doctors listened to her heart
with their stethoscopes, satisfied.
Nurses took blood, gave tests;
the word was, she's doing ok.
Not one of them checked her eyes for a pulse.

# Skeleton

Imagine after death,
the flesh melted off
you're speeding thru
blackest earth so fast it looks white
every bump thunders off bone
resounding blast of cymbals,
all this crazy music
where once, eyes, ears, nose
snowwind flies thru, as
you plunge head first
80 miles an hour back
into your own skin:
the sun shining
Gold!

**SOMETHING IS BURNING IN BROOKLYN**

Poems by **LINDA LERNER**

# Something Is Burning in Brooklyn

on Court Street
fire engines rush down
crowded lunch hour streets
people look up
a tension squeezing second grabbed
out of an hour like the few dollars
stashed from paychecks
for the day   **that day**  happens again
*the fire   where is the fire* someone shouts
heads pivot toward the court building
people rub their eyes


nothing and no time to squeeze out
another sour tasting second
hungry for something sweet and
worn out looking for the fire
*I think I smell smoke* someone shouts
everyone freezes: smoke from
that Bronx fire that killed
so many in the time it takes to light up
an outlawed cigarette
lingers in the air   but
isn't *this* fire we can't see
burning thru our boro…

rushing thru each other
thru another Brooklyn week
feel its heat rising fast as our rents
as a new Manhattan blazes
in real estate mogul's heads
a fast as our grocery bills
*$21.00 and nothing to eat*
she says
        and she and he
if   only we could

# Art Found

climbing up cable wires
knocked loose by a storm
on one side of a cement slab
separates renovation work
from where I live
brought down trees   ungreened a garden
to green the new owner's property
I'd called Time Warner to complain about
whose promises fell thru the cracks
way people do in
upbeat gentrification times
cracks ivy rose up from
greened & thickened around the wires
in the worsening dustnoise
I opened my window
to yell out when
              a vision
...a giant green   *up yours* finger
sticking it to the destroyers
took my breath away

# Just a Cat's Breath Away

...struggling  her way out
Spanish into English out of Guatemala
to come where she's lived for years
Marie keeps it simple....
nothing about the accident that took
her young husband's life
left her to raise five kids alone—
*it's ok*, she smiles, always smiles
the screen behind which she changes,
lets herself in if I'm out
if I can afford to have her clean
trusting her with the keys
as I would have my own mother
but never did...

my cat, Samsara, I call him sam,
knows her by the smell he picks up
brushing past; first time
she arrived before I left

he ran after me to the door
fear flashing in his green eyes
that hurled me back decades:
a Brooklyn tenement stoop I sat on crying
after my mother left my father
"for good"she screamed
would continue to scream till
she watched the words she couldn't take back
shoveled over his coffin

fear I'd be raised by my old world father
of losing the one person who keeps a world
from being destroyed
                    ...just a cat's breath away
from what would happen/does

a writer in his mid eighties told me
when the bomb was invented everyone thought
the world would end soon...
forty years later in a hospital room
by his daughter's side waiting
for a liver to be delivered that
didn't come in time,
then...it happened then...

drills once sent us rushing under desks for cover
protected us only from fear...and only one kind;

Sam clings to my assurances,
*I'll be back* what
Marie's husband must have cried
out the door into the car before it
smashed thru her world

*see you soon   love you*
last words inhaled whenever someone lights up....
I should scream, *please don't...*
*it isn't only your life*
but the smoke that took a life
returns it slowly enters my body
every part, yes like that   and JUST like that
is snuffed out   and I smell the ashes...
but oh, those few grateful moments

250

# The Distance Between Two Points

born on a back road-street
to 1930s depression parents

born in an irishman's bed
while my father said kaddish for me
born when I took off more than clothes
saw myself for the first time
in my lover's eyes & fell in love

born an immigrant's daughter
whose father couldn't find the exit off
                              a back road
I'd choose: gypsy   artist   a sidewoman
playing word gigs...

33 westminster road:
quiet block with a fancy name
nobody thought about
in that other brooklyn where I grew up
not park slope's hipster place
or gang ridden poor

weren't any projects people feared walking past
mostly catholic church going
working class people who got by
a few jews like me
who wanted to be like the others
                              not OTHER
before I knew
the distance between a back road
& the main one can't always be solved...

argyle road around the corner
where I played & one day
lost beating a car to the other side
laid up all summer in my father's
anger-blame   blinded me to his fear...
church avenue the main drag,
cortelyou   beverly   road-streets
a three room apartment
in an old walkup
with a linoleum carpeted living room
one fitted over the other
one fixed in memory...

a dumbwaiter rode up & down
our evenings picking up garbage
                        and gossip
roaches in the tub secrets
fights we were forbidden
to let run out open windows
my mother's pride slammed shut
hiding my father's business failures
a cashier in waldbaum's   never
made it to manager but
kept us off welfare   his kids thru college
only couldn't keep her warm in bed or out...

after his operation told her, "it's all right
if you want to with someone else..."
too late for my mother to hear...

my brother   silent unbothered
inside that place I never found
mapped on the other side of where

252

I'd be born & born again
in the same house as he

full birth   a luxury
we couldn't afford then
I can't not afford now

to say what doesn't begin with choice
ends with it   to say
having been unable
to get off the road I was born on
is where I belong
becomes choice
that the distance between two points
can always be measured
the uncertainty principle rules physics
not a life...to believe
where I am is where I want to be

is to pretend at the speed of light
forget I'm stuck on earth
that to love someone who died
means I've already died once
—omitting the kaddish death
that the time for being bornagain
may end before
the desire for it

# After Reading Jack Wiler on a Full Moon Night

and thinking about my latest rent increase
moving to a cheaper apartment
where I don't want to live
or taking a trip to India
I move from the living room to the bedroom
consider getting more work
to pay for what it won't next year/
India sounds better...
try not to think of
my lover who reneged
on his "forever" promise by dying
look for what we had elsewhere
even if it doesn't exist
we didn't have all of it anyway
although we did
& move to the window
consider going out later
to look at the stars
imagine what it's like to be
Jack Wiler looking at the stars
be like my lover who can't see them

...once in Taos, New Mexico,
a friend drove me to the Grand Canyon
I stood at the edge peering down
a car   tiny like a child's toy
smashed at the bottom...
I wondered if there were people
skeletal remains inside
how easy it would be to slip
stared at it as I'm now staring

at a world that could end any moment
the what if/in case poverty/illness
a fanatic's heaven explodes
death at my doorstep again

I move to the kitchen
a hunger for what I can't name   to find...
one time visiting a friend in another city
told to walk west from the train station
then turn left till I came to a rite aid
and head north to some grocery
around the corner from a mcdonalds
across from a pizza shop
or was it laundromat & walk diagonally
down the chance
I'd find my way out
& get to her house—

I look up at the stars
guiding me nowhere/everywhere
& the moon that crazy sky balloon
floating out of my head:
I could burst it
just like that   I think
like this: not moving anywhere
nowhere at all

# The Persistence of Memory

*from a painting by Salvador Dali*     7/25/06

July comes round like Dali's
four melting clocks

I spring out of hot morning showers
            to towel dry
apply the lotion he can't wait to lick off
                        or I to feel
his scratchy tongue up my legs

Yes it's like that & this
            and even
the little bit I stop him from
triggering every nerve

four years since
you tongued me out of a death
            took you
melted down like it was nothing

an alchemist's lost trick
stumbled on in a bathroom
my cat fooling with
your baby's bodymind
on a hot July day like the one
four years ago you
            vanished
                in

# Driving America

*for Lowell Scheiner*

a large white convertible cruises
into late December, turning heads,
a few rub their eyes, "wow, neat car,"
someone yells, another gives a thumbs up
to the white haired man behind the wheel;
                    he nods back,
just taking his baby out for a spin,
not wired to twenty first century sound bytes
no seat belts to strap him in
                    It's 1959.  His first car.
"aint nothin' but a hound dog" rocks;
just out of college and ready to make news
he's burning rubber in Brooklyn
the country still riding *I love Ike*
prosperity, victory in not
just one but future wars;

what would have paid
kids'college tuition, bought a nice home
keeps his engine running, heart beating:
50 years and good as new,
but every creak in the car's struggle
to push open its top echoes in his bones
means it's back to finding a mechanic
knows how to fix classic cars
won't rip him off;
price doesn't matter: in this car
he's lost nothing

driving down Flatbush Avenue toward
a sign that reads Atlantic
crosses another avenue back to
the mom & pop owned Brooklyn
of small grocery stores, drugstore counters

he sat at sipping egg creams, feeling
like he was standing in the outfield
at Ebbets Field ready to pitch into greatness,
back on that old route 66, reaching
skyward across the American imagination,
down streets barbershop poles twirl
red white and blue's possibilities;

people stop walking, stare
or peer out small car windows
from cost of gas, high rent & job worries
their own era's annihilation threats
roaring overhead to where
the Armageddon didn't happen
bomb the Russians never dropped,
stare at this shiny new-looking Ford
James Dean or Elvis might have driven
top pulled down waving to the crowd,
stare in wonderment; almost prayer...

two women in jeans, stiletto heels
rings in their noses, lips,
*bring the troops home* buttons on
jackets point to the car,
"it rocks" one shouts, he looks out,
abruptly rear ended by 2008;
"hey mister," the woman cries,
"if you're going to Williamsburg,
can you give us a lift?"

## Isn't It Always When

the concrete gives way
/something miraculous
as when walking down union street one day
the sidewalk turned to metal
bridging over dirty green water
and thinking it must be polluted
must be the gowanus everyone
is desperate to clean up
say is bad for us
and probably are right
but I like this unruly looking place
around which deals are being made
in a frantic land grab to hi rise
two/three story houses
smooth out a neighborhood's rough edges
like it as
I like the rumpled sweaty disarray
left from lovemaking
to the clean virtual kind
like this crazy block of
shut down factories
graffiti scrawled all over the wall
of an abandoned building
steps leading to a padlocked door
outside a small balcony
no concrete facts to support it
weeds growing up every which color way
like Whitman's wild children
blossoming rebellion just on
on the other side of the bridge
I'd already crossed over
preferring the stink I can smell
to the one I can't...

# Appendix 1
## Notes on Poems

17—Takes Guts and Years Sometimes
The poet referred to is Diane de Prima.

27—Following a Professor into Blues Waters...
"Have you ever loved a woman" —from "Everybody Has
Their Turn" sung by Gatemouth Brown.

It's hard but it's fun/life may break your little heart/baby
oh baby/please don't feel so bad/makes daddy feel so/bad
/baby oh baby...—as sung by Lightnin' Hopkins

53—For Leo Connellan, Unfinished Business
All quotes, unless otherwise indicated, are from Leo Con-
nellan's poems

The reference to "Cherry Alive" is from a poem by Delmore
Schwartz

140—A Nod to Dylan Thomas
Reference to the poet & quote (in italics) is to Jack Mi-
cheline.

143—Poem for America's Unofficial Poet Laureate
Walt Whitman quote from "Poets to Come."
Allen Ginsberg quote from "Plutonium Ode."

171—In Soldier Slang

my eyes burned holes
thru the jungle,
looking for death, hoping
to see it before
it saw me...

Quoted from Andrew Gettler letter, March 2000.

173—A Koan for Samsara
Samsara—The wheel or ocean of life and death, wheel
of time…cyclic existence or round of birth and death and
rebirth within the six realms of existence, characterized by
suffering, impermanence and ignorance.

Koan—A problem that has no intellectual solution; the
answer has no logical connection with the question, meant
to baffle the intellect.

176—From the Fire
Triangle Shirtwaist Factory Fire on March 25, 1911

"still a down and
    further still to fall and faster than i
      thought…"

Quoted from "Liquid Jesuit" by Andrew Gettler.


178—An Off the Wall Protest

Long Bình Jail's—largest military stockade in Vietnam.

"wanting is the hottest sweetest thing you know"

"love at first sound" by Andrew Gettler

181—The Bowery and Other Poems

"…When old souls connect…
You were never gone, I was never alone"

Quoted from Andrew Gettler.

205—What's Missing    Is
Typer—Bukowski's name for the typewriter.

235—And the Bones Pile Up
Both quotes are from "replacements" & "dark decade" by
Andrew Gettler published in *Footsteps of A Ghost* (Iniquity
Press/Vendetta Books).

# Appendix 2

## Acknowledgments

## *Grateful Acknowledgments*

### New and Uncollected Poems

"Takes Guts & Years Sometimes" appeared in *Alpha Beat Press,* July 1999; "The Insult of Good Intentions" appeared in *Chiron Review,* Winter 2008; "Riding On a Late Night Amtrak Back to New York From Philly" appeared in *New Verse News,* January 16, 2008; "Visions of Outlaw Ghosts" appeared in *Last Call: The Legacy of Charles Bukowski* (Lummox Press, 2004); "Here's The Catch" appeared in *Danse Macabre;* "What Won't Die Easily" appeared in *The Long-Islander* (Walt's Corner), October 29, 2009; "Following a Professor Into Blues Waters Stalls on Dry Land" appeared in *Clockwisecat,* November 2007; "What Remains" appeared in *The Haight Ashbury Literary Journal,* 1998; "See I Told You" appeared in *New Verse News;* "The Enemy" appeared in *Home Planet News,* Fall 2008; "The Period Keeps Receeding the Harder She Tries to Reach it & the Closer She Gets" will be in a future issue of *The New York Quarterly;* "Building In the Green" appeared in *New Verse News;* "City Streets" appeared in *Chiron Review;* "Only One" appeared in *BigCityLit,* 2009; "The Scream" appeared in *Poets4Haiti;* "Fault-lines" appeared in the *Brownstone Poets* 2009 Anthology; "Mid East Sand Blows Thru Katz's Deli New Year's Day, 2010" appeared online in *Rusty Truck;* "Define Freedom Try" will be in a future issue of *Phoenix 4.*

### For Leo Connellan

"For Leo Connellan" appeared in *Home Planet News,* Spring 2002.

### *City Girl*

"Risking," "All Us Casualties" and "City Rain" first appeared in *The New York Quarterly,* issues, 46, 48, and 59, respectively; "This Was The Year" appeared in *Black Buzzard Review,* 1988.

## No-One's-People

"Sixty" appeared in *The Signal*, Vol.V, No. 1.

## She's Back

"Old People At TheBank" appeared in *Slipstream*, 1991; "I Said Yes" appeared in *Caprice*, March 1992; "She's Back" appeared in *Bouillabaisse*, 1992; "Knowing the Difference" appeared in *Cover Arts New York*, February 1994; "Going Down" appeared in *North Stone Review*, No. 11, 1993; "You Listened, Remember" appeared in *Die Young*, Summer 1993; "Mugging" appeared in *Flaming Envelopes*, 1993; "Price on Our Heads" appeared in *Grist On-Line*, January 1994; "Played Jazz Violin Like An Out of Town Junkie" appeared in *Pudding*, 1995; "A Ghost's Progeny" appeared in *Register Citizen*, July 17, 1994; "Protest" appeared in *Big Hammer #6*.

## New & Selected Poems

"The Other Couple" appeared in *Register Citizen*, January 8, 1995; "What I Miss" appeared in *Alacran* (The Maverick Press, 1996); "For Survival" appeared in the *Wisewomen's Web*; "Men Called Jack" appeared in *Thunder Sandwich*, March 2000.

## Anytimeblues

"Blizzard '96" appeared in *Graffiti Rag*, 1996, "Bluespoet" appeared in *Main Street Rag*, 1996; "Poem For America's Unofficial Poet Laureate" appeared in *Home Planet News*, Autumn 1997; "When The Holy Man Came" appeared in *Pudding*, December 1997; "What It Comes Down To" appeared in *S.L.U.G. Fest, LTD*, Autumn 1997; "A Nod to Dylan Thomas" appeared in *Rattle*, Summer 1999; "Bluespoet" appeared in *The Lucid Stone*, Spring 1997; "Because You Can't

I will" appeared in *One Trick Pony*, 1995; "When an Editor Praising My Poems Asks But Why & Do You Have Any That Are More" appeared in *Green Bean Press*, 1999; "Farewell to a Downtrodden Saint" appeared in *Nexus*, 1998, and in the *Ragged Lion Anthology*, 1999.

### No Earthly Sense Gets It Right

"Imagine the Sound of One Hand Clapping" appeared in *Chiron Review*, Summer 2000; and in *Cortland Review*, on-line issue 6; "Spontaneous Rant" appeared in *zzz zyne* (JVC Books).

### Greatest Hits (1989–2002)

"Construction Summer" appeared in *Blue Collar Review*, Summer 2001; "Haywire" appeared in *Lummox*, 2002.

### A Koan for Samsara

"Resurrection: Easter 2000" appeared in *Poetz.com*, October 30, 2000, and in *Big Hammer*, issue 6; "From The Fire" appeared in *Black Bear Review*, Summer 2003; "An Off the Wall Protest" appeared in *Poems for Peace* at *Poetry* online; "In Soldier Slang" appeared in *Big Scream*, 2004; "A Well Travelled Ghost" appeared in *The Louisanna Review*, 2000, and *NYCPoetry.com*.

### The Bowery and Other Poems

"Brooklyn Unmapped" appeared in *Home Planet News*, Summer 2000; "One of the Ten Best" appeared in *Parting Gifts*, 2004; "On Meeting Ray Bremser" appeared in *Lucid Moon*, Feburary 1999 and in *Cosmic Baseball Association*, online,1999), "What Is It About" appeared in *The Underwood Review*, 1999; "The Bowery" appeared in *poetry.about.com*; "One of the Ten Best" appeared in *Parting Gifts*, 2004.

## Because You Can't I Will

"The Rare Soul" appeared in *poetry.about.com*; "I Call Him Sam" appeared in *Rogue Scholars Press*, 2004; "Street Jazz/ Blues thru Summer Hot" appeared in *Poesy*, 2006; "Once Only for Sailors and Hotshots on Motorcycles" appeared in *Poets Wear Prada*, 2005.

## City Woman

"The Gateway" appeared in *City Lore* (www.cityofmemory. com); "Chicago" appeared in *Dufus #6*, Lummox Press, 2006; "Retro 20th Century Ghost" appeared in *Van Gogh's Ear*, 2006; "TriBeCa Blues a Migrant Blues" appeared in *Lost Highway* (Blues Poetry Anthology), Lummox Press, 2000.

## Living In Dangerous Times

"The Good German" appeared in *Main Street Rag*, 2005; "And The Bones Pile Up" appeared in *Big Scream*, 2007; "I Am Asked to Believe" appeared in *Paterson Literary Review*, 2003; "The Fall" appeared in *Onthebus*, 2005; "Skeleton" appeared in *Chance of a Ghost Anthology* (Helicon Editions, 2005)

## Something Is Burning in Brooklyn

"The Distance Between Two Points" and "After Reading Jack Wiler On a Full Moon Night" appeared in *Big Scream*, 2008; "The Persistence of Memory" appeared in *Nomad's Choir*, Fall 2008; "Just A Cat's Breath Away" appeared in *Shabdaguchha*, 2008; "Isn't It Always When" and "Something Is Burning in Brooklyn" appeared in the *Brownstone Poets*, 2008; "Art Found" appeared in the *Brownstone Poets*, 2010; "Driving America" appeared in *New Verse News*, 2008.

# Appendix 3
## Blurbs

## City Girl

*City Girl* is wonderful...I hope this poet continues going.
—Leo Connellan

Linda Lerner's poems are finely written and very appealing....
—Diane Wakowski

## She's Back

If you had not read Linda Lerner's poems you would be deprived of her uniqueness, her individuality, her special insights about life.... She evokes Russian ancestry, womanhood, motherhood, essential sorrows and joys, "Brooklyn Streets." She is specific about her feelings and gives an urgent sense of reality.

Linda Lerner offers her truthful increment to the voices of new poets in our land. She enriches the richness of current American poetry, part of a grace of new young oncomers.

—Richard Eberhart

## New & Selected Poems

As a city dweller in the latter 20th century, with bridges burning behind her, Linda Lerner observes the war wounded, the capsized, the hidden victims of internal and perpetual murder & refuses to be burnt out. Like wildflowers in a vacant lot, her poems bear witness. She reports with exactitude on friends and lovers cutting through the *merde* of this world. She extends a hand. She maintains the wry humor of a survivor.

—Janine Pommy Vega

## A Koan for Samsara

Some of the most passionate, sexiest love-poems I've ever read. And without doubt some of the most piercing poems of grief. It's a profoundly moving selection. Beyond skill and technique, the natural work of a fully mature artist who has absorbed her whole training and experience.

—Hayden Carruth

## Living in Dangerous Times

Linda Lerner should be one of the most visible of our poets in this country...she is in a special outsider group of powerful and original American poets largely ignored by Poetry Establishment forces. Her amazing energies zap her poems with high voltage.

—Robert Peters

## City Woman

Linda Lerner's City Woman bristles with all the discordant energy, jump-cut quickness, gritty urgency, and vibrant color of a great city brought to life on the printed page by a fine poet able to hear, in the midst of the urban throb, the beating of the human heart.

—W. D. Ehrhart

### Something Is Burning in Brooklyn

Linda Lerner is a poet who bravely articulates the emotions
of fear and loss on both a personal and universal level. The
conflict between the alienation of a big anonymous city
and the need of the individual for meaningful experience
provides the tension in her work.... Her m/o is New York
colloquial with a hipster edge. The city images are precise
and crisp reflecting a keen perception. From "Driving
America":

       two women  in jeans, stiletto heels
rings in their noses, lips,
bring the troops home buttons on
jackets point to the car,
"it rocks" one shouts, he looks out,
abruptly rear ended by 2008;
"hey mister," the woman cries,
"if you're going to Williamsburg,
can you give us a lift?"

Lerner's work ranges from gritty to the edge of sentimental,
occupying the linguistic borderland between Street and
Beat with tough but feminine sensibility.

—Eric Greinke

# *About the Author*

Linda Lerner is a New York City Poet, born and raised in Brooklyn where she now lives.

She is the author of thirteen poetry collections and has been twice nominated for a Pushcart Prize. Her most recent collections are: *Something Is Burning in Brooklyn* (Iniquity Press /Vendetta Books, 2009), *Living In Dangerous Times* (Presa Press, 2007), and *City Woman* (March Street Press, 2006). The last two were Small Press Reviews' Pick of the Month. In 1995, she and Andrew Gettler founded *POETS on the Line* (http://www.echonyc.com/~poets) the first poetry anthology available on the Internet. For Nos. 6&7 (1997/1998), the Vietnam Veterans/Poets issue, she received a 1997 Puffin Foundations Grant & Ludwig Vogelstein Grant. *POETS on the Line* will be kept permanently on the Net, though it ceased publication with the Millennium issue (Nos. 9&10). Her poems have appeared in *The New York Quarterly, Louisiana Review, Paterson Literary Review, Onthebus, Van Gogh's Ear, Home Planet News, BigCityLit, Chance of a Ghost: An Anthology of Ghost Poems, Ragged Lion: A Tribute to Jack Micheline, Big Hammer,* and *Danse Macabre* among others.

# *About NYQ Books*™

NYQ Books™ was established in 2009 as an imprint of The New York Quarterly Foundation, Inc. Its mission is to augment the *New York Quarterly* poetry magazine by providing an additional venue for poets already published in the magazine. A lifelong dream of NYQ's founding editor, William Packard, NYQ Books™ has been made possible by both growing foundation support and new technology that was not available during William Packard's lifetime. We are proud to present these books to you and hope that you will continue to support The New York Quarterly Foundation, Inc. and our poets and that you will enjoy these other titles from NYQ Books™:

| | |
|---|---|
| Barbara Blatner | *The Still Position* |
| Amanda J. Bradley | *Hints and Allegations* |
| rd coleman | *beach tracks* |
| Joanna Crispi | *Soldier in the Grass* |
| Ira Joe Fisher | *Songs from an Earlier Century* |
| Sanford Fraser | *Tourist* |
| Tony Gloeggler | *The Last Lie* |
| Ted Jonathan | *Bones & Jokes* |
| Richard Kostelanetz | *Recircuits* |
| Iris Lee | *Urban Bird Life* |
| Kevin Pilkington | *In the Eyes of a Dog* |
| Jim Reese | *ghost on 3rd* |
| F. D. Reeve | *The Puzzle Master and Other Poems* |
| Jackie Sheeler | *Earthquake Came to Harlem* |
| Jayne Lyn Stahl | *Riding with Destiny* |
| Shelley Stenhouse | *Impunity* |
| Tim Suermondt | *Just Beautiful* |
| Douglas Treem | *Everything so Seriously* |
| Oren Wagner | *Voluptuous Gloom* |
| Joe Weil | *The Plumber's Apprentice* |
| Pui Ying Wong | *Yellow Plum Season* |
| Fred Yannantuono | *A Boilermaker for the Lady* |
| Grace Zabriskie | *Poems* |

Please visit our website for these and other titles:

**www.nyqbooks.org**

www.ingramcontent.com/pod-product-compliance
Lightning Source LLC
Chambersburg PA
CBHW032038080426
42733CB00006B/118